Envoy Extraordinary

Malcolm Muggeridge
&
Alec Vidler

HARPER & ROW, Publishers
New York, Evanston, San Francisco, London

Contents

List of Illustrations

Rome

Sea of Adria

Neapolis

MACEDONIA

Thessalonica

Beroea   Apollonia

Rhegium

SICILY

ACHAIA   **Athens**

Syracuse   **Corinth**
Cenchreae

MALTA

Mare Internum

Paul's Journeys

1st   ⟶

2nd   ⟶

3rd   ⟶

To Rome ▬▬▬▬

Pontus Euxinus

Philippi
Neapolis
apolis
Samothrace

Troas
Assos

Pergamum

BITHYNIA

GALATIA

PHRYGIA

Aegean

ASIA

Ephesus

Miletus

Sea

Laodicea
Hierapolis
Colossae

PISIDIA

Antioch (Pisidian)

Iconium

Lystra
Derbe

CILICIA
Tarsus

Cnidus

RHODES

Attalia
Perga

Antioch
Seleucia

CRETE

Salamis

SYRIA

Orontes

Paphos
CYPRUS

Sidon
Damascus

Tyre
Sea of Galilee

Caesarea

JUDEA

Alexandria

Jerusalem

ARABIA

Nile

100 miles

St Paul being mocked by his audience. A tenth-century illumination of a codex in the monastery of St Gallen.

VARIATIONS ON
A THEME

*There has probably seldom been anyone at the same time hated with
such fiery hatred and loved with such strong passion as Paul.*
A. DEISSMANN

It always does me good to see a man enjoying St Paul. J. DENNEY

In my student days there was a German professor who used to
interrupt his enthusiastic exposition of the Apostle with the inter-
jection, 'Aber, meine Herren, dieser Paulus war ein feiner Kerl' (he
was a fine fellow).
J. OMAN

What sort of man was Paul? – Not by any means a saint. Goodness
was far from being his most notable characteristic. He was proud,
unbending, imperious; he was self-assertive and masterful; he used
hard words; he believed that he was absolutely right; he stuck to
his opinions; he quarrelled with may people. E. RENAN

The sojourning of Paul in any place was no ordinary thing.
CHRYSOSTOM

Luther once, when asked how he envisaged the appearance of the
apostle Paul, answered with an affectionate guffaw, 'I think he was
a scrawny shrimp-like Melanchton'. R. BAINTON

Paul: Christ's second eye. AMBROSE

11

L'embauché, Saül Paulus, c'est-à-dire Saül le Petit, était un terrible petit homme, un esprit de feu dans un corps d'avorton, un timide audacieux, un chétif orgueilleux, un faible qui brandissait une force divine, un malade infatigable, un gueux qui conquérait le monde.

P. L. COUCHOUD

To the historian there must always be something astounding in the magnitude of the task Paul set himself, and in his enormous success. The future history of the civilised world for two thousand years, perhaps for all time, was determined by his missionary journeys and his hurried writings.

W. R. INGE

In the whole range of literature there is nothing like St Paul's letters. Other correspondence may be more voluminous, more elaborate, more studiously demonstrative. But none is so faithful a mirror of the writer.

J. B. LIGHTFOOT

St Paul's Epistles read like good conversation.

B. JOWETT

Wheresoever I open St Paul's epistles, I meet not words but thunder, and universal thunder, thunder that passes through all the world.

J. DONNE

Cardinal Bembo, Pope Leo X's friend, refused to read the Epistles of St Paul, lest, he declared, they should contaminate his Ciceronian Latin.

S. REINACH

No one understood Paul till Marcion, and he misunderstood him.

A. VON HARNACK

The man who, I suppose, did more than anybody else to distort and subvert Christ's teaching was Paul.

A. N. WHITEHEAD

I have not got to listen to St Paul because he is clever, or even brilliantly clever; I am to bow before St Paul because he has divine authority.   S. KIERKEGAARD

St Paul would almost certainly have condemned tobacco if he had known of its existence.   S. BUTLER

The spiritual strength of Paul springs from the fact that he lives in two worlds; not only in the visible world of change and decay, of tears and death, that world in which we are 'afflicted in every way' and 'perplexed', but also in the invisible world in which there is no fear and no despair.   R. BULTMANN

To the man who longs for God and cannot find him; to the man who wants to be acknowledged by God and cannot even believe that he is; to the man who is striving for a new imperishable meaning of his life and cannot discover it – to this man Paul speaks.

P. TILLICH

I hold St Paul to have been the first great corrupter of Christianity.

J. S. MILL

Men have cried for one hour of Socrates . . . Oh, much more for one hour of the great Apostle to smite with his flaming sword of sincerity and truth.   C. GORE

Would not St Paul come along . . . and to my breezelessness bring his breeze – his breeze of faith!   H. MELVILLE

St Paul was wrong about sex.   BISHOP JAMES PIKE

In the scholastics I lost Christ but found him again in Paul.

M. LUTHER

When Paul – the arch-enemy of Jesus, his people and mankind – is removed from the entrance of the kingdom of God, the door will reopen.   O. MICHEL

I do not want to be a philosopher if the price of it is that I must rebel against St Paul. ABELARD

Christ was an Aryan. But Paul used his teaching to mobilize the underworld and to organize an earlier Bolshevism. A. HITLER

The real Paul has been half buried under a Talmud of Paulinism.
W. R. INGE

A god who died for our sins: redemption through faith: resurrection after death – all these are counterfeits of true Christianity for which that disastrous wrong-headed fellow, Paul, must be held responsible. F. NIETZSCHE

Paul is . . . the 'professor' among the Apostles. THOMAS AQUINAS

Paul the apostle . . . deserved to be admitted into the mysteries of the third heaven, yet his ears were boxed by the angel of Satan.
ERASMUS

It was Paul who converted the religion that has raised one man above sin and death into a religion that delivered millions of men so completely into their dominion that their own common nature became a horror to them, and the religious life became a denial of life.
G. B. SHAW

> How oft, when Paul has serv'd us with a text,
> Has Epictetus, Plato, Tully, preached!
>
> W. COWPER

Especially make yourself familiar with Paul. Him you ought to hold ever in your heart, 'day and night he should dwell in your hand', and his words you should commit to memory. ERASMUS

Paul, what a man he must have been! K. BARTH

14

What Jesus preached was a new birth of the human soul; what Paul preached was the ancient religion of priest and altar and the propitiatory bloodshed.   H. G. WELLS

It would be no loss to exchange the theological literature of a whole generation of later epochs against a single Epistle of St Paul.....
                                                                 LEO CHESTOV

Paul was a rabbi in intellect and an apocalyptic in feeling.
                                                                 O. SPENGLER

It is frankly disappointing to see how Paul hardly ever allows the real Jesus of Nazareth to get a word in.   C. G. JUNG·

Dudley Moore and Peter Cook

DUD

I think St Paul's got a bloody lot to answer for.

PETE

He started it, didn't he?

DUD

All those letters he wrote.

PETE

To the Ephiscans.

DUD

You know, 'Ah, dear Ephiscans, ah, stop enjoying yourself, God's about the place'.

PETE

'Signed Paul.' You can just imagine it, can't you? There's a nice Ephiscan family, settling down to a good breakfast of fried mussels and hot coffee, and they're just sitting there, and it's a lovely day outside, they're thinking of taking the children out, ye know, for a picnic, by the sea, by the lake and have a picnic there, and everything's happy, the sun coming through the trees, birds are chirping away.

PETE

DUD
Boats bobbing on the ocean.

PETE
The distant cry of happy children.

DUD
Clouds scudding across the sky.

PETE
Naturally, Dud – in fact an idyllic scene is what you call it, when suddenly into the midst of it all – tap, tap, tap, on the bloody door.

DUD
What's that?

PETE
You know what it is?

DUD
No.

PETE
It's a messenger bearing a letter from Paul. They rush to the door to open it, thinking it may be good news – perhaps grandfather's died and left them a vineyard. They open it up and what do they discover? 'Dear George and Deirdre and family, stop having a good time, resign yourself not to have a picnic, cover yourself with ashes and start flailing yourselves.'

DUD
'Till further notice.'

PETE
'Signed Paul.'

A LETTER TO A
FRIEND

Dearest Alec,

The only way I can introduce this transcript of our conversations about Paul as we followed his missionary journeys is by way of a tribute to a long friendship. It was in the autumn of 1920 that I first set eyes on you; at Selwyn College, Cambridge, where we were both undergraduates, you in your last year and I in my first. The three years' difference in our ages showed a good deal more then than it does today, when, apart from your venerable beard (a subtle form of camouflage you now affect), it shows scarcely at all. I was seventeen, straight from a government secondary school and an ardently socialist home; you had been just old enough to serve and get a commission in the wartime army, had taken a first and shown yourself to be a good all-rounder at games, still in those far-off days a necessary adjunct to being well regarded in Cambridge colleges. We could scarcely have been more different in background, standing and aspiration. As an ordinand and a pillar of the Junior Combination Room, a public-school boy well furnished with caps, colours, oars and other impedimenta of distinction, you belonged to a world I had only read about in *Tom Brown's Schooldays*, not to mention those illustrious publications the *Magnet* and the *Gem*. It never occurred to me that so lordly a figure would even nod in my direction. When I found that you were actually prepared to accord me your friendship, I was more flattered and delighted than I perhaps let on; an excess of egotism has always made it difficult for me to admit an obligation in any human relationship, and anyway, according to socialist categories, you belonged to the mighty who were to be put down from their seats rather than to the humble and meek due for exaltation.

I can very easily see you now as you were then; dark, of course, instead of white, but already with the serenity, the air of having an inward life into which you could and did repair for a substantial part of each day, that characterized you when you were an undergraduate, as it still does. Whenever I hear Luther's famous hymn, *Eine feste Burg ist unser Gott*, I think of you; for me, you have always been a stronghold sure. How often during the half century of our friendship I have found in this strength of yours ballast to steady my own too often rudderless, surf-riding existence. This despite long periods of physical, and sometimes intellectual, separation. Apart from the ultimate intimacies of love, friendship is, in my experience, the best thing life has to offer. The very fact that it is, in the most absolute sense, disinterested, seeking neither egotistic nor sensual ends, sets it apart from other relationships. In friendship I consider I have been particularly blessed; most of all in yours.

Nothing, of course, could be nicer from my point of view than your present retirement to your old house at Rye some ten miles from where I live. Thus we find ourselves, you in your seventies and I nearing them, enjoying the same delightful intimacy as in our undergraduate days. Paying visits to one another, going for walks, talking over books we have read and experiences we have had; altogether, in a desultory way, taking stock of what Wordsworth calls 'the heavy and the weary weight of all this unintelligible world'. The house is very much as I remember it on my first visit, in the summer vacation of 1921. Then, the first-floor room, now your library, was used by your mother for her book-binding; she sat there, as I remember her, among the litter of her occupation, looking very much as you do among your books. The view from the garden over the marshes to the sea is unchanged; the family importing business, whose premises down by the Strand had the same sort of fascination for me as Peggotty's house in an upturned boat at

Yarmouth had for David Copperfield, has disappeared, but one looks out through your front windows at Rye Church, with its splendid flying buttresses, standing as solidly as ever. Nearby is Henry James's house; on that first summer visit it was occupied by E. F. Benson, who later sat majestic in the Mayor's Chair at morning service, previously occupied by your father.

In the subsequent years I have followed your career mostly from afar – as a parish priest in Newcastle and Birmingham, at St Deiniol's Library at Hawarden, at Windsor and at King's College, Cambridge – but always with sufficient intimacy to be able to summon up a picture in my mind of what you were doing and how you were living. If you had been worldly or ambitious, without a doubt you could easily have grasped one or other of the major prizes still available to clerics; most people who know you, or have come within the range of your influence, would agree that you are one of the most – if not the most – considerable figure among contemporary Anglicans. I never met anyone more remote from such considerations, less interested in matters of status or money or celebrity; though, as is characteristic in my experience of the truly unworldly, with a perfect awareness of the gradations and diversities of men. Egalitarianism is a form of vanity; in God's family, as in our human ones, there is not so much equality as a oneness.

This aloofness of yours from worldly considerations is also, from my point of view, a very favourable circumstance. It means that we are both, as it were, washed up for our last years on a remote and desert shore. When my insatiable ego, however many times struck down, once more lifts its cobra head, I can look to you for help in emulating the philosopher in *Rasselas*, and endeavouring 'to abstract my thoughts from hopes and cares which, though reason knows them to be vain, still try to keep their old possession of the heart; expect, with serene humility, that hour which nature cannot long delay, and hope to possess in a better state that happiness which here I could not find, and that virtue which here I have not attained.'

How delightful, then, that in these agreeable circumstances the chance should arise of embarking together on a project that had been vaguely in my mind ever since I was involved as commentator in making three television programmes on the Life of Christ. This was to participate similarly in making a series of programmes on the apostle Paul. I knew that I could never undertake the requisite commentary alone, and equally that finding a suitably equipped scholar prepared and able to collaborate with someone as ignorant and opinionated as myself would be an almost impossible task. Then the thought arose that you might do it, and, further, that, if you were willing, we might make the commentary a running dialogue between the two of us. You did agree, and I was over-joyed. It was a wonderful opportunity to go on a fascinating journey in your company, in the process exploring together the thoughts, achievements and insights, the whole complex persona, of this remarkable man who began by malignantly persecuting the followers of Christ, and then became his most splendid advocate, missionary and envoy extraordinary to the whole pagan world.

It was all very appropriate as a matter of fact. To you I owed my first true acquaintance with the Christian religion. What more fitting, then, than that half a century later I should be guided by you in coming seriously to grips with the founding father of Christendom? Before I got to know you at Cambridge, Jesus had been to me a notable figure in my father's pantheon of great idealists and social reformers, and Paul, the prototype of all priests, the legalist who transformed Jesus's joyous ministry into an institutional Church and his gospel of love into a recitable creed. I have lived to see this view, then considered highly unorthodox, if not outrageous, become incorporated in the contemporary conventional wisdom, not least in influential ecclesiastical circles. It was through you that I began to understand that Christianity was a great drama rather than a mere set of enlightened values, a beneficent ideology; a drama whose climax, the crucifixion, followed by the resurrection, held out the hope, not just of living in a better way, but of being reborn into a new creation. This was something that I stored away in my mind, and often forgot and ignored, but never quite lost. It belonged particularly to the two terms I spent with you at the Oratory House in Cambridge, when I had a taste of the sweet regularity of the religious life, with its periods of silence, and successive offices, and afternoons spent working in the garden with Wilfred Knox, and the evening angelus. A brief oasis of order in a disorderly life.

So, one way and another, it was a great moment for me when we started off on our travels, first, in the company of Peter Chafer, our producer-director, making a reconnaissance tour of the places Paul visited and preached in, and then, having joined up in Jerusalem with Ken Macmillan, our brilliant cameraman, and his crew, retracing our steps to do the actual filming. I had been rather apprehensive about how you would react to the tedium and inescapable fraudulence of holding forth in front of the cameras, since you had, of course, no previous experience of anything of the kind. I need not have worried. Where I feared your patience might be strained, it was mine which gave out. Wearing a white floppy hat of the kind that used to be favoured by prep-school boys, carrying your essential books in a haversack, once, I should suppose, used to contain a gas-mask, equipped with a small cushion to mitigate the asperities of sitting on rock faces and other uncomfortable perches, you discoursed at and with me in total disregard of the weird antics of our crew and the often frantic gestures of our director. Not even being thrown by your donkey (alas, out of vision!) disturbed your equanimity; you confused Greek professors in Athens with an ease Paul himself might have envied, and handled the arrayed élite of the Turkish Information Service at a banquet in Izmir as to the British Council born. On that particular occasion, to your great satisfaction, I was addressed as 'Count', the reason being, as we discovered afterwards, that the Turkish authorities had received a telegram from their embassy in London announcing my arrival, but without saying who I was. As no one in Izmir, or for that matter in Turkey, had ever so much as heard of me, it was decided that, having no other distinction, I must have a title to justify the attention lavished upon us.

I am a poor sightseer, and soon weary of archaeological remains. Already in my memory Ephesus and Caesarea and Corinth and Philippi and Troas are indistinguishable heaps of fallen masonry and rubble. This, incidentally, led to one of our sharper exchanges – at Pisidian Antioch, where I ventured to remark that I find travelling about Asia Minor and the Middle East, where every step taken is in the dust of some forgotten civilization, for this very reason particularly pleasurable. My point was that in such circumstances all the pretentions of historians are automatically laid low; the historical past they try so hard to reconstruct is visibly obliterated, whereas Paul's words, handed down to us in what many regard as quasi-mythical records, ring out louder and clearer than ever. You would not have it so, of course; the historian, you insisted, also labours in the vineyard of truth, helping to signpost the way that a Paul sees in a blaze of light on the Damascus road, and thenceforth proclaims. It was a difference which, in one form and another, cropped up on numerous occasions, and one that I have pondered over endlessly. The truth that transcends the fact; the myth more real than reality; the Word that exists in the beginning before there are tongues to speak it and minds to remember and record it, and that goes on existing when the tongues and the minds and all their records have likewise passed away. An historical Jesus contained in the dimensions of time, and a transcendental Jesus bridging the gulf between eternity and now; making eternity now and now eternity.

Paul himself, in any case, as we both agreed, was very much a figure of history. An incorrigibly mortal man in the Falstafian sense. He soon joined us on our travels; someone very solid, substantial, energetic, covering prodigious distances, presumably for the most part on foot, staying sometimes for longer or shorter periods with one or other of his congregations, but mostly on the move. Along those long, long roads, some of which, like the Via

Egnatia, have survived to this day including the very paving-stones he trod on. Without a home, or even a room, to call his own; his books and manuscripts, his very clothes, scattered here and there. Plying his trade of tent-maker (whatever precisely that may have been), thereby jealously guarding his independence, in accordance with his own dictum that unless a man works he shall not eat.

His real work, of course, was telling everyone who would listen to him about the birth, ministry, death and resurrection of Jesus Christ, the so long expected Messiah. We followed him from synagogue to synagogue, at each of which he had been well received as a recognizable rabbi, and then been chased out when he moved inexorably on from expounding the scriptures to proclaiming the coming of Christ's kingdom, and the realization it brought of the glorious liberty of the children of God. One of the synagogues, at Beroea – I'm sure you remember it as vividly as I do – was so ancient, and on the identical site of the one Paul actually held forth in, coming there from Thessalonica, that we almost expected him to loom into view. A small, bald, bandy-legged, big-nosed man (I was happy that you were inclined to accept that second-century description), who sometimes had the face of an angel. I could easily guess what some, at any rate, of the occasions for this transformation must have been; surely his amanuensis will have recalled how brightly his face shone when, in the midst of dictating polemics, admonitions, instructions of one sort and another, he suddenly broke off into one of those truly sublime utterances of his –

Though I speak with the tongues of men and of angels . . . Who shall separate us from the love of Christ? . . . But the fruit of the Spirit is love, joy, peace, longsuffering . . .

– which belong not only to the highest flights of mysticism, but also to the greatest literature of all time.

Reading Paul's letters over and over with you, I fell completely in love with them, coming to see belatedly that, from any point of view, they are among the most remarkable documents to come down to us from antiquity. How, hurriedly dictated, as they must

23

have been, at odd moments, they yet convey with astonishing vividness and verisimilitude the whole character and circumstances of the early churches and the first Christians. They came to seem in my eyes a kind of sublime journalism; transcendental reporting of the very highest order – the kind that Blake engaged in when he stepped out of the world of time to survey with a painter's careful exact eye the eternity that lay around it. What comfort for me, too, in that directive to the Christians at Colossae to *let your speech be alway with grace, seasoned with salt, that ye may know how ye ought to answer every man!* Who that has ever tried, however inadequately, to reach up with words to the mystery of things will not echo Paul's prayer for a door of utterance, *to speak the mystery of Christ . . . that I may make it manifest as I ought to speak?* The words were, to me, the more wonderful because they were so patently not studied, but poured out just as they came, presenting, I daresay, some difficulty to whoever had the task of transcribing them. That the letters were thus composed seems to me to be abundantly clear in the very choice of words and structure of the sentences. Take, for instance, the categories in the famous passage about what may separate us from the love of Christ – *tribulation, or distress, or persecution, or famine, or nakedness, or peril, or sword;* then the succeeding list of the ones that assuredly will not be able so to separate us – *neither death, nor life, nor angels, nor principalities, nor powers, nor things present, nor things to come, nor height, nor depth, nor any other creature.* Is it not obvious that these, so arbitrarily yet marvellously chosen, come, as it were, warm and inspired, straight from his mouth rather than being first chosen and arranged in his mind?

Inside Paul the mystic, providing that other face – shrewd and calculating, if not crafty – there was the Pharisee, preoccupied with Old Testament prophesies and all the multitudinous intricacies of the Law, as he had studied it under Gamaliel and expounded it as a young man with great brilliance to the admiration of his elders. The same mind which had led him to persecute the Christians so relentlessly functioned after his Damascus road experience no less

energetically and masterfully on their behalf. It is the contrast between
these two sides of his nature that made him, while he was alive, and
subsequently, so complex and controversial a figure. We found it
most interesting, and at times diverting, to assemble some of the
divers opinions which have been expressed about him. Our assembly
could have been far more extensive; there is scarcely a single
questing soul in the last two thousand years who has not at one time
or another expressed an emphatic opinion about Paul.

The opinions, as will be seen from our selection, vary enormously;
he is a man about whom no final judgement ever has, or, it is safe
to predict, ever will, be reached. One of those unique men who
defy all categorization and all tabloid assessments. I remember
discussing this with you on the roof of St Peter's in Rome, as we
looked down at the vast concourse of people making their way
across the piazza and up the steps into the church which has so long
been the centre of the Christendom Paul, as Christ's emissary, may
be said to have founded. What would he make of the scene, we
asked ourselves, without finding a clear answer, and went on to
wonder whether it was this very enigmatic quality in him which
accounted for the paucity of statutes and pictures of him compared
with other apostles which we had noticed in Rome. Did the very
artists draw back from committing themselves to a representation
of such a man?

Certainly, we never lacked for a theme; I really believe we could
have gone on talking about him almost indefinitely, as we might
have spent far more time than the two months at our disposal
following him on his restless journeys from city to city, up and
down the highways and the seaways of the great Roman Empire as
it existed in his time. One conversation that sticks out in my mind
with particular clarity was at Paphos, in the ancient basilica
adjoining the ruins of the residence of the Roman proconsul, in
Paul's day Sergius Paulus. There we discussed the burning topic,
more than ever crucial today, of what a Christian owes to Caesar
and what to God; standing side by side in those tall narrow stalls

like upturned coffins that you find in Greek churches, while the bearded priest brought in green boughs in preparation for Easter.

There was a time when I should have regarded it as almost blasphemous to fall in with Paul's insistence that all earthly authority, even the Emperor Nero's under whose dispensation, as a Roman citizen, he perforce lived, must be regarded as coming from God, and that whoever resists such authority automatically puts himself at enmity with God. Now, conscious of belonging to a society visibly falling apart, morally and in every other way, I can see more clearly what he meant. What a difficult balance to strike between the exigencies of order and of freedom! You, who care as little for authority as anyone I have ever known, can still see clearly why Paul felt bound to commend even the shaky corrupt rule of a Nero as providing some sort of scaffolding for the ramshackle edifice of public order in an already decomposing Roman Empire. Subsequently, I had the same discussion with Enoch Powell, the two of us this time occupying the twin pulpits in the beautifully restored Wren church of St-Mary-le-Bow. He – assuredly no hater of authority – saw the dilemma from Caesar's side, and wondered how anything could be salvaged from his exigencies to give to God. My own impulse is so strongly the other way that every Caesar and commissar who ever was or is to be seems stuffed with straw.

Paul, in any case, in forming his estimate of what was due to Caesar had the great advantage of believing that the millenium was near, and the curtain about to fall for ever on our human scene. Such a prospect, as you justly remarked, quoting Dr Johnson on a man about to be hanged, wonderfully concentrates the mind. There would be little point in throwing Nero to his own lions, even supposing such an enterprise to be otherwise desirable, if in the near future the heavens were going to unfold like a scroll and the Son of Man appear in all his glory riding on a cloud. Furthermore, most of Paul's flock were slaves with no stake in the Roman State anyway, so that the notion of overthrowing, or bettering, it would have had little appeal, especially in the light of the lasting liberation through Christ that Paul proclaimed. A congregation of slaves convinced that the world must soon end would seem to constitute the ideal progenitors of the Christian religion. Today we have plenty of slaves; all that remains is to persuade the Archbishop of Canterbury, the Cardinal Archbishop of Westminster, the Moderator of the General Assembly in the Church of Scotland and one or two others that the millenium is near. This should not be too difficult.

The readiness in Paul to accept any secular authority on any terms doubtless accounts in part for his unpopularity today, when all change is considered to be for the better, and each new acceptance of servitude is hailed as liberation. Actually, it is the very gospel he did so much to propagate which has offered, and continues to offer, the only basis there is for being free at all in our mortal condition; as is exemplified in his enchanting Letter to Philemon, which I first read with you beside Lake Eğridir, and now almost know by heart. The runaway slave is sent back to his master as an act of restitution, but with this admonition: *That thou shouldest receive him for ever; not now as a servant, a brother beloved, specially to me, but how much more unto thee, both in the flesh and in the Lord.* As he dictated these words, far more than any Spartacus uprising, Paul made the institution of slavery inconceivable in Christian terms, even though twenty centuries later, in our own time, when chattel slavery had been abolished, new variants, racial, economic and ideological, were to make their appearance and claim their millions of victims.

Another aspect of his present unpopularity is undoubtedly his attitude to marriage and sexual indulgence, which we discussed at Cenchraea, one of the ports of Corinth, dabbling our feet in the sparkling water of the Mediterranean there. It was a problem which must have posed itself with particular urgency – how were Christians to be induced to live chastely or virtuously in a society as permissive and decadent in its time as ours is. Paul called upon them, in their new-found freedom, to eschew the vices and debaucheries which were going on around them, reminding them in the magnificent eighth chapter of his Letter to the Romans that to be *carnally minded is death, but to be spiritually minded is life and peace.* No doctrine could be less acceptable today, not only to the many who have turned away from Christianity, but also to many ostensible Christians, including ministers and priests and bishops. Among the divergent opinions about Paul, we quote the late Bishop Pike's that he was 'wrong about sex'. The remark was made to me as we walked amicably together out of a BBC Television studio. It echoed in my mind when I read of his tragic death in the desert near Jericho.

The maintenance of Christian standards in so inimical a moral climate which Paul required of Christians was not possible through mere observance of the Law; he had tried this himself, and almost been destroyed in the process. It could only come through grace; the rebirth which had befallen him on the Damascus road, followed by his emergence as a new man. Of all the things I learnt with you in our Pauline travels and discussions, I value most this clear distinction between the Law with its necessary definitions, and the new dispensation of love which Christ instituted in the world, and confirmed with his death and resurrection. The Law sufficed to sustain the synagogues as citadels of virtue in a decadent and declining civilization, but Christ's dispensation of love provided the light of hope and joy and creativity out of which a new one would be born. If now this new one is in its turn waning, the light is still there; as when Paul first took it from Jerusalem to the Hellenistic world, in the process transforming what might have been merely a Judaic cult into a universal religion.

I must say the moment when, at the behest of the mysterious man from Macedonia, he decided he must go to Europe, was for me the most dramatic of all. We stood, you will remember, on a hill at Troas looking out at the sea he crossed, and then on another hill at Kavalla, in his day Neapolis, watching the boats come in, as it might have been his. What a truly momentous occasion that was, and, like all the most important events, passing largely unnoticed, human beings in all ages having a wonderful faculty for becoming preoccupied with what matters least and averting their eyes from what matters most. So he pressed on, we hot on his heels, until we reached Athens, where, on Mars' hill, we fell into a somewhat acrimonius dispute about whether the philosophers who gathered there to listen to Paul were more like dons or journalists, I, not surprisingly, inclining to the former view, and you to the latter. Whether dons or journalists, we could agree that they were very like their twentieth-century equivalents, with their passion for always *telling or hearing something new*. There was so much in Paul's world to remind us of ours; like the demo at Ephesus when the mob shouted monotonously for two hours on end: *Great is Diana of the Ephesians*, or, for that matter, the games, with their presentation of spectacles of violence and eroticism for the edification of multitudes of listless viewers.

It is a curious thing, but in retrospect it seems as though I took my leave of Paul, not in Rome where he was martyred, but at Miletus where he said goodbye to the elders of the church in Ephesus, and then went on to Jerusalem to grapple with the always rather cantankerous church there, and to hand over the money he had so assiduously collected for them from his mostly Gentile congregations. The events in Rome are only vaguely in my mind, but this parting at Miletus is as vivid to me as though I had been one of the elders myself. Do you remember that we both agreed that we sensed Paul's presence more strongly than anywhere else in that desolate stretch of marshland, once Miletus's busy harbour, where the sea had receded – rather like Romney Marsh. Perhaps it was the virtual absence of ruins and of tourists, perhaps the very desolation and remoteness of the place, but as you read his speech to the elders about how they would see his face no more, and how he commended them to God and the word of his grace, I felt like joining them in weeping sore and falling on his neck. So I shall always think of him there, on that moving occasion, so resolute, so eloquent, so faithful a servant of Christ; desperately needed then in the world of round about 50 A.D., and as I think, and I know you do, too, no less desperately needed today, in the world of the nineteen seventies.

MALCOLM MUGGERIDGE

THE CONVERT

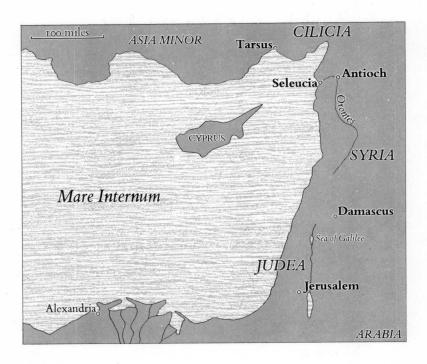

THE CONVERT

Introduction

PAUL was born about the beginning of the Christian era at Tarsus, in what is now southern Turkey. It was a much more important and attractive city then than it is today. Son of a Jew who was also a Roman citizen,[1] for which reason he was given the Roman name 'Paul' as well as the Jewish name 'Saul', he was well brought up, and was sent to Jerusalem to complete his education. Indoctrinated by the rabbis and impelled by his own zealous nature, he became an earnest and ardent exponent of the strictest form of Judaism, and so took an active part in persecuting the recently formed sect which made the preposterous claim that Jesus of Nazareth, who had died a criminal's death, was the long-awaited Messiah.

All the same, Paul could not help being deeply impressed by the steadfast conviction and serene courage displayed by these Christians when they were beaten up. His encounter with the Christians, together with the frustration he experienced in his attempts to get right with God, prepared the way for the turning-point in his life – his vision and conversion on the road to Damascus. The bright light that flashed upon him at that crucial moment was to make him

1. Roman citizens were exempt from certain kinds of punishment and had a right of appeal to Caesar. See Acts 16: 37 ff.; 25: 11 f.

33

an 'envoy extraordinary' of the faith which hitherto he had despised and fought against.

After a period of reflection and preparation he was soon taking a decisive and leading part in the course of events that transformed the Christian movement from a small Jewish sect into a new community open to all peoples and nations. It was from Syrian Antioch, the first great centre of Gentile Christianity, that Paul set out on the tireless and hazardous journeys which were to issue in the foundation both of a universal Church and of a civilization that still survives, though its future is now gravely imperilled.

At Tarsus

MALCOLM

I must say it's a funny chance, Alec, if one looks back to fifty years ago when we were undergraduates together, that we should now find ourselves in Tarsus, looking for St Paul! Of course during these fifty years not only have you been my dearest and oldest friend, but also you have been studying the New Testament, studying Paul's epistles; you're a theologian, you're an expert. I can't claim to be anything of that kind. But in a way it may give me a certain advantage. At least I shall come freshly to these extraordinary documents which I'm quite convinced are among the most luminous ever written in the history of the world.

ALEC

I agree about that, and I take it that we also agree that, after Jesus, Paul is the key figure in the whole Christian story.

MALCOLM

Yes: Jesus was the light and Paul spread the light.

34

MALCOLM

I understand that in Paul's day Tarsus was a thriving port and a great city with a big university.

ALEC

It was indeed a great centre of learning and philosophy: famous on that account among the cities of the time. Some said that it was more distinguished than even Athens.

MALCOLM

Though Tarsus today is very different from the Tarsus Paul knew, in which he grew up and went to school – it's come down in the world – still the mountains to the north of the city remain the same, the contours, the hills, the river, and all the rest of it. Even so, I can't help feeling that to look for Paul, a man who belongs to the very beginning of the Christian era, in Tarsus as it is today and in this twentieth century, is extremely difficult.

ALEC

That's very true, but I would say that at any period it has been prodigiously difficult to understand this extraordinary man. Nevertheless, it's endlessly worthwhile to try to get at the truth about him, and I'm expecting that our attempt to follow the course of his life will reveal much more about him than I have so far realized.

MALCOLM

I suppose that Paul as a Jewish boy, and the son of an orthodox Jew, would have lived with his fellow Jews in a special quarter of the city.

ALEC

Probably so, but not in a ghetto. They will have had plenty of commercial and other dealings with the Gentiles among whom they lived. That is to say, they couldn't keep themselves to themselves, or have the kind of exclusive or enclosed life that the Jews had in their homeland in Palestine. The Jews in Tarsus and in the other cities around the Mediterranean were known as the Dispersion (or Diaspora), because they were kind of colonies of Israel scattered or dispersed from their mother country.

MALCOLM

Wasn't Paul's father a Roman citizen as well as a Jew?

ALEC

Yes, and no doubt the whole family much prized that fact as well as their being descendants of Abraham and members of the tribe of Benjamin.

MALCOLM

There is one thing, Alec, I particularly want to get clear. What was the essential difference between the hellenized Jews of the Dispersion like Paul and his family and the Jews of Judea?

ALEC

The primary difference was that they spoke Greek which was the common language of the Roman Empire, whereas the Jews in Jerusalem normally spoke Hebrew or Aramaic which was a sort of modernized form of Hebrew. But there was of course more to it than a difference of language. The Jews of the Dispersion were naturally influenced by the non-Jewish environment in which they lived. They not only spoke Greek but to some extent adopted Greek ways of thinking. So far as they could, they shared the life and entered into the activities of their fellow citizens, while at the same time they drew the line at anything that involved idolatry or compromise with paganism or moral laxity.

MALCOLM

I presume that though Paul usually spoke Greek he would learn Hebrew in the course of his education.

ALEC

Undoubtedly: but he was brought up on the Septuagint,[2] that is on the Greek translation of what we call the Old Testament and Apocrypha. This was, so to speak, the text-book on which his education was based, and it provided his daily mental and spiritual food. Nearly every paragraph he wrote and every speech he made reflects his intimate familiarity with his Greek Bible.

MALCOLM

What about the social status of Paul's family? Does the fact that he became a tentmaker indicate that his origins were what we call working class?

ALEC

There are some interesting points about that. One is that the Greek word translated 'tentmaker' in our English versions probably had a wider meaning in Paul's time such as 'leather-worker'. So his father may have had quite a prosperous business in the leather trade, and as a lad Paul might for a time have been, as it were, apprenticed to the business. On the other hand, it seems unlikely that he was a manual worker by upbringing. Do you remember that in one of his letters he

2. The Septuagint (commonly denoted by the symbol 'LXX') is so called because of the (legendary) tradition that the translation was made at Alexandria by seventy-two elders in seventy-two days.

seems to pride himself on 'working with his own hands'?[3]

MALCOLM

Yes, I see: no born manual worker would say that. The one desire of the man who really has to work with his own hands is not to do so much longer. In any case I suppose it is difficult to relate the social status of Paul's family to our social conditions today.

ALEC

The most we can say is that they were probably what in our terms would be a middle-class family.

MALCOLM

One thing is obvious. Paul's father must have been well enough off to send him to Jerusalem to complete his education and to have the famous rabbi Gamaliel as his teacher.[4]

In the streets of Jerusalem

MALCOLM

What exactly did it signify, Paul's going to Jerusalem to be trained as a Pharisee? Did that mean being a rabbi?

ALEC

I should say that, if he hadn't been converted, he would have become a famous rabbi and have outshone Gamaliel himself. But as regards the general question, we have to bear in mind that in the Judaism of that time there were various schools

3. I Corinthians 4: 12.
4. Acts 22: 3.

and parties, notably the Sadducees and the Pharisees who are well known to us by name because they figure so much in the Gospels. I think they correspond rather to what used to be called in England the 'broad churchmen' and the 'high churchmen'. The Gospels aren't altogether fair to the Pharisees. They were extremely good people as well as being extremely religious, very strict and conscientious in all their concerns. Their devotion and piety were centred on the Law, or the Torah as the Jews called it. The Torah doesn't mean legislation, but divine instruction or teaching. What they believed was that God through Moses and the prophets had revealed to men the best way of living, both as individuals and as a community: a way of living that was pleasing to God and that was for the well-being of man. This is what the Law or Torah meant to them.

And they regarded it as a tremendous boon and blessing, as indeed it was. When you consider the moral anarchy of the permissive societies by which they were surrounded, you can see why they delighted in the Law. They loved it. That very long psalm, 119, is all in praise of the Law, and contains expressions such as 'thy statutes have been my songs in the house of my pilgrimage'.

MALCOLM
But what about the Sadducees?

ALEC
They were comparatively easy-going and accommodating in their religion, and much less rigorous in their interpretation of the Law and its demands. They wanted to have the best of both worlds. Most of us, I fancy, would have found the Sadducees more congenial than the Pharisees – though I

don't say that you would have, Malcolm! Anyhow, Paul was a Pharisee and had no use for the Sadducees.

MALCOLM

His training as a Pharisee under Gamaliel must have affected his whole state of mind and his spiritual development.

ALEC

It certainly did. The strict piety of the Pharisees, based on the Law, if taken really seriously could have two kinds of effect. On the one hand, the more the requirements of the Law were elaborated in detailed rules and regulations, the more burdensome the whole thing became, the more difficult to comply with completely; and so it was frustrating. A man felt: it's hopeless, I can't get right with God by carrying all this out, it's beyond me. On the other hand, the more successful a man was in keeping the Law and its ordinances, the more pleased with himself he was liable to become. He got the idea that he was putting himself right with God by his own efforts, and that he was being justified by his own self-centred achievements. And this was precisely the frustrating impasse in which Paul eventually found himself and from which he was to yearn for some release.

MALCOLM

That explains his perpetual return to the subject of the Law and to the way in which the new revelation in Christ brought

---

1 *'Jesus was the light and Paul spread the light.'* (p. 34)

2 *'Though Tarsus today is very different from the Tarsus Paul knew . . . still the mountains to the north of the city remain the same . . .'* (p. 35)

3 *'This ancient church, built on to a cave at the foot of Mount Silpius on the outskirts of Antioch, is said to be the site of the first Christian church building.'* (p. 52)

deliverance from it. I can see that it arose from the terrific indoctrination in the Law that he received in Jerusalem.

ALEC

For the Jews, and especially for the Pharisees, the Law, the Torah, was the beginning and end of their faith. Everything hung on it. So, when they found that the Christians seemed to be calling the whole thing in question, nothing could have been better calculated to bring out the fury and fanaticism in a young Pharisee such as Paul was at this time.

MALCOLM

Wasn't Paul's anti-Christian fanaticism concentrated on Stephen? What sort of a man was he?

ALEC

Stephen was a Greek-speaking Jew who emerged as a leading spokesman of the Christians in Jerusalem.[5] He started a new style of teaching and preaching, in which he severely criticized the traditional Jewish attitude to their own history, to the Law and the Temple. He even went so far as to say that, in rejecting Jesus, they had been true to form; they had been doing that all through their history – rejecting their prophets, and so on.[6]

MALCOLM

A very explosive thing to say.

ALEC

Infuriating.

MALCOLM

But of course very much what Paul himself was going to say later on, wasn't it?

5. Acts 6.   6. Acts 7: 51 f.

ALEC

Later on, yes, but the very obverse of what he'd think of saying at this time. Paul was apparently a leading spirit in the agitation against Stephen.

MALCOLM

And they did what always seems to have happened – called out the mob.

ALEC

I doubt if it needed much calling out. Mobs seem automatically to gather together when a thing like this arises, don't they?

MALCOLM

Indeed they do, and they readily produce the necessary slogans and incitements to violence. Isn't it said that they gnashed upon Stephen with their teeth?[7]

Outside the walls of Jerusalem

ALEC

It was through the gate, which is still known as St Stephen's Gate, that he was pushed with this mob at his heels, eager to see him condemned and out of the way.

MALCOLM

I suppose stoning is about as horrible a way of dying as you could possibly imagine. And not only for the poor victim, but for the people throwing the stones, which is bestial and

7. Acts 7: 54.

loathsome. And what about the spectators, the people looking on?

ALEC

In some ways it was worse in their case, because they'd
nothing to do except to gloat over it.

MALCOLM

And among them, consenting to it as we're told, was Paul.
Whatever can he have felt as he saw this man, this heroic man,
dying? Doesn't the Acts of the Apostles bring out the contrast
between the abominable cruelty of the mob and the wonderful serenity of Stephen as he died?

ALEC

This is what it says:

> ... they cried out with a loud voice and stopped their ears and
> rushed together upon him. Then they cast him out of the city and
> stoned him; and the witnesses laid down their garments at the feet
> of a young man named Saul. And as they were stoning Stephen,
> he prayed, 'Lord Jesus, receive my spirit.' And he knelt down and
> cried with a loud voice, 'Lord, do not hold this sin against them.'
> And when he had said this, he fell asleep.[8]

MALCOLM

This experience of being present at Stephen's execution by
stoning must have had a tremendous effect on Paul.

ALEC

I think it got under his conscious mind and nagged and
haunted him continually. How could anyone who was
spiritually sensitive be unaffected by the serenity and courage
of Stephen's faith, however much he might try to suppress
his feelings about it?

8. Acts 7: 57-60.

MALCOLM

After all, Paul didn't regard the Christians as harmless. He regarded them as evil, as people who should be extirpated, and yet he had to face the fact that their way of looking at life produced in Stephen this heroism of a very unusual kind.

ALEC

And no doubt every time afterwards when Paul was beating up other Christians who showed a similar serenity and courage, this would remind him of the traumatic experience of Stephen's martyrdom, and would drive it home more and more.

On the Damascus road

MALCOLM

Some time after Stephen's stoning, Paul took the road to Damascus, which leads by Galilee. His purpose in going there was to ferret out any of the Jews who were being influenced by the Christian teaching. For this purpose didn't he get some kind of credentials from the Sanhedrin?

ALEC

According to Acts he got authorization from the high priest.[9]

MALCOLM

Paul does seem to have been an insatiable persecutor.

ALEC

This doesn't surprise me, because after all he was a man of ardent, indeed fiery, temperament, and whatever he did, persecuting or anything, surely he'd do it with all his might.

9. Acts 9: 1 f.

MALCOLM

I suppose so. But it was on the road to Damascus that the great decisive experience of his life took place, so mysterious to understand or to convey.

ALEC

Its supreme importance is shown by the fact that there are three accounts of it in Acts, which differ only in minor details. The one in Chapter 26 is perhaps the best.

> *. . . I journeyed to Damascus with the authority and commission of the chief priests. At midday . . . I saw on the way a light from heaven, brighter than the sun, shining round me and those who journeyed with me. And when we had all fallen to the ground, I heard a voice saying to me in the Hebrew language, 'Saul, Saul, why do you persecute me? It hurts you to kick against the goads.' And I said, 'Who are you, Lord?' And the Lord said, 'I am Jesus whom you are persecuting. But rise and stand upon your feet; for I have appeared to you for this purpose, to appoint you to serve and bear witness to the things in which you have seen me and to those in which I will appear to you, delivering you from the people and from the Gentiles – to whom I send you to open their eyes, that they may turn from darkness to light . . .'* [10]

MALCOLM

Conversion is something that you as a priest must have met with often – a person being reborn, becoming a new man. Paul is said to have been blinded by the experience,[11] but he was blind only because afterwards he truly could see whereas before he couldn't.

10. Acts 26: 12-18.
11. Acts 9: 8 f.

ALEC

Paul's conversion does seem to have been sudden, but of course sudden conversions are seldom as sudden as they seem. I remember reading somewhere that our twentieth-century psychologist Jung had remarked that Paul had been a Christian for a long time before his conversion, only unconsciously.

MALCOLM

You mean fighting against something he knew would ultimately captivate and capture him.

ALEC

That's the idea. Jung added that fanaticism of the kind Paul had been displaying is nearly always a compensation for secret doubt.

MALCOLM

After this extraordinary experience on the Damascus road Paul naturally wanted to get away and be alone.

In the desert

ALEC

In one of his letters Paul describes how after his conversion he went off on his own so as to be able to reckon with the consequences of what had happened to him.

> . . . *when he who had set me apart before I was born, and had called me through his grace, was pleased to reveal his Son to me, in order that I might preach him among the Gentiles, I did not confer with flesh and blood, nor did I go up to Jerusalem to those who were apostles before me, but I went away into Arabia.*[12]
> 12. Galatians 1: 15-17.

Arabia, that means the desert. Even today, anybody who has had a shattering experience wants to get away somewhere to sort it out in quietness and solitude. And in the Bible nearly everybody who had a great experience did this – Moses, Elijah, John the Baptist; Jesus after his baptism went into the desert. It is natural that Paul should do the same. Practically all his earlier beliefs had been turned inside out. For instance, until now he'd thought of Jesus as a dead pretender, but now he was absolutely convinced that he was the living Lord, the centre of a new creation, a new world, which was going to make everything different for him.

MALCOLM

I was going to ask you about that, because he's always talking about being 'in Christ'.

ALEC

Yes, he uses the expression again and again. It means, I would say, that Christ was, as it were, the new atmosphere in which he was going to live and breathe and which he was always going to depend upon. And he wanted everyone else to live in this atmosphere and to breathe it.

Then again, the cross was absolutely different for him now. Up till now the idea of a crucified Messiah had been an intolerable scandal, but now he was convinced that on the cross the Son of God had given himself for him and had saved him from the frustration in which he'd been trying to put himself right with God through doing the works of the Law and by earning merit. What he saw now was that God had taken the initiative in Christ and with amazing generosity had accepted him as an adopted son, just as he was, despite his abject unworthiness, and without his having to sweat

47

away to get right with God by his own self-centred efforts. He had only to put his whole trust in what God had done for him in Christ and then to live out his life in thankfulness for that.

MALCOLM

Paul knew that this light had shined on him not only for his own sake; he must shine in the world. So there was no remaining in the desert for him. He must go out into the cities and on to the roads and meet his fellow men, carrying this light with him.

ALEC

It was like a torch that had been handed to him and that he'd got to carry to everybody else – though at this stage of course he had no idea how he was going to be able to do it.

MALCOLM

So this extraordinary man in one flash understood what truth was. And then, through his time in the desert, understood what the rest of his life had got to be dedicated to, and he did dedicate it – undeviatingly.

On Mount Silpius, overlooking Syrian Antioch

ALEC

Some time after he emerged from his retreat in Arabia, Paul tells us that he went to 'the regions of Syria and Cilicia'.[13] He was there, it seems, for several years going about visiting the synagogues and witnessing to his new-found faith.

13. Galatians 1 : 21.

MALCOLM

Tarsus was in Cilicia, and it was there that Paul was found when he was wanted at Antioch in Syria. One can see from this mountain site what a marvellous city Syrian Antioch must have been. Wasn't it the third city in the Roman Empire?

ALEC

Yes, with a very large population, which included a great many Jews. So there will have been several synagogues.

MALCOLM

And then these Jews were joined by the Jewish Christians who, after the persecution following the stoning of Stephen, had had to leave Jerusalem.[14]

ALEC

We've also got to take into account the Gentile sympathizers in Antioch who, here as elsewhere, were attached to the synagogue. They valued the high moral standards of Judaism and attended synagogue services, but didn't want to become Jews because of the requirements of the Law about circumcision, food regulations, etc.

MALCOLM

I believe they were known as 'god-fearers'; men and women in a sort of no-man's-land between paganism and Judaism.

ALEC

Altogether, we can see that the situation at Antioch was pretty complex, and could easily give rise to trouble.

14. Acts 11: 19.

MALCOLM

From the point of view of the apostles in Jerusalem it must
have been confusing and possibly dangerous.

ALEC

Quite so. They evidently heard about it and were somewhat
alarmed. So they sent Barnabas, one of their most trusted and
tactful leaders, to take stock of the situation.

MALCOLM

What led him to seek the help of Paul?

ALEC

He probably felt that he was confronted by a situation that
was more than he could deal with by himself. Paul was an
old friend of his; he'd originally introduced him to the older
apostles,[15] and he'd heard of his missionary work in Syria
and Cilicia. Paul seemed to be just the man who could help
him to take stock of the situation at Antioch.

MALCOLM

We're told that Barnabas 'brought' Paul to Antioch. That
word 'brought' rather interests me. Nowadays it would be
quite simple of course, although even now it's a long drive,
as we know, from Tarsus to Antioch; but then it must have
been quite a complicated undertaking to fetch someone like
that.

ALEC

One would think so, all that distance. I suppose they were
used to it and didn't set much store by it.

15. Acts 9: 27.

MALCOLM

It was impossible for Barnabas to alert Paul that he was coming.

ALEC

No telephones, you mean, or telegrams.

MALCOLM

Yes, I mean there were no means of communicating promptly. Anyhow, he brought Paul to Antioch, and the two of them were there to sort out the situation and report back, presumably to Jerusalem, about it.

ALEC

Paul's relations with the apostles at Jerusalem are by no means clear. The documentary evidence on the subject in the New Testament is inconsistent. Paul certainly paid some visits to Jerusalem, but the number and timing of them is doubtful. At some stage, when he was there, he came to an agreement with Peter as the chief of the original apostles, that they would look after the mission to the Jews, while he and Barnabas would be free to be responsible for the mission to the Gentiles.[16]

MALCOLM

Those are the sort of arrangements that sound very simple and easy but in fact often don't work out at all well, and I suppose there was trouble over this one.

ALEC

There was, to be sure. It was at Antioch that the problem of Gentiles wanting to become Christians without taking on the

16. Galatians 2: 9.

Jewish Law came to a head. There was a lot of friction and controversy before Paul succeeded in establishing his position, and we shall hear a good deal more about it.

At the oldest church in Christendom

MALCOLM

This ancient church, built on to a cave at the foot of Mount Silpius on the outskirts of Antioch, is said to be the site of the first Christian church building.

ALEC

It's not an unreasonable claim. In the cave behind the present building the Christians of Antioch may well have met for worship in those very early days.

MALCOLM

So if there is one place where you could say that the story of Christendom as distinct from the story of Christianity began, it would be Antioch in Syria. The real issue, Alec, as I see it, was this. Was Christianity to be a universal religion or a Judaic cult? Paul's heart was wholly on the side of its being a universal religion. And so the mainspring of his life was fixed here in Syrian Antioch. It was here that for the first time a Christian church existed as a separate entity from the synagogue. Logically enough too, it was from here that the first Christian missionaries, Paul, Barnabas and John Mark, set forth down the river Orontes to Seleucia, the port of Antioch, and on from there to Cyprus and the world.

THE CHRISTIAN

THE CHRISTIAN

Introduction

FROM Seleucia in Syria Paul and his companions sailed to Salamis on the east coast of Cyprus, near the modern seaside resort of Famagusta. The ruins of Salamis, which was a large and handsome city, are still being excavated. Barnabas was a native of Cyprus[1] and John Mark was his cousin,[2] so there was probably a happy family reunion soon after the ship berthed. The fact that they already had friends there will have contributed to the favourable reception that awaited Paul in the synagogues at Salamis.[3]

After some weeks, the missionaries travelled to the other end of the island, passing on the way the beauty spot known as 'Aphrodite's Bay',[4] where according to legend she sprang from the foam of the sea. They were making for Paphos which was the seat of the Roman governor, and Paul had a memorable encounter with him.[5] All this time, Paul the convert was doubtless not only enriching his own understanding of the Christian faith but also becoming quite clear

1. Acts 4:37.
2. Colossians 4: 10.
3. Acts 13: 5.
4. The Greek goddess Aphrodite was called Venus by the Romans. Cyprus was one of the principal centres where she was worshipped. It was in fact called 'Aphrodite's Island'.
5. Acts 13: 6-12.

in his own mind that he must press on to preach the gospel to Gentiles as well as Jews.

It was this determination that led him and Barnabas to cross to the mainland. They landed at Attalia, the chief port of Pamphylia. After a brief stay at Perga, which was a few miles inland, they decided to strike up country through the mountain tracks with the Roman colony at Antioch in Pisidia as their goal.

At Salamis

MALCOLM
Though Paul was now as passionate a Christian as he'd been a passionate persecutor of Christians, he was still a Pharisee. As such he continued to be received in the synagogues of the Dispersion. It was these expatriate Jews who were the first target of his missionary zeal. With Barnabas and John Mark he made for Cyprus on what was in effect his first missionary journey. As they approached the island they will have seen Salamis, as voyagers now see Famagusta. When Paul arrived here, it was a large and prosperous town and port, wasn't it?

---

4 *'Arabia, that means the desert.'* (p. 47)

5 *'Some time after Stephen's stoning, Paul took the road to Damascus, which leads by Galilee.'* (p. 44)

6 *'So they sent Barnabas, one of their most trusted and tactful leaders, to take stock of the situation.'* (p. 50)

ALEC

I should call it a city. If it had been in England today, it would have had a Lord Mayor.

MALCOLM

And then had a Roman governor, because it was a province of the Roman Empire.

ALEC

Salamis wasn't the capital of the island at this time, though it was to be later on. The governor lived at the other end of the island at Paphos.

MALCOLM

As Paul had Barnabas with him, and Barnabas was a Cypriot, I presume that they naturally met people whom they already knew.

ALEC

Barnabas' family probably lived here, and so there will have been a family reunion as soon as it was known that the ship was coming in. A happy time for all was in prospect.

MALCOLM

With plenty of old associations and with a large Jewish community here?

ALEC

There certainly was. The Jewish historian Josephus records that Caesar Augustus made Herod the Great a present of half the copper mines in Cyprus and committed the care of the other half to him.[6] So a lot of Jews had come here to work.

6. Jospehus, *Antiquities of the Jews*, Book XVI Ch. iv §5.

MALCOLM

What an astute and enterprising man this Herod was! Getting in on this copper production is rather like the British government's taking a share in BP.

ALEC

Or Disraeli's getting a share in the Suez Canal.

MALCOLM

Naturally the Jews working and living here had established synagogues and they had their usual community life.

ALEC

We know from the Acts of the Apostles there was more than one synagogue.[7] Very likely there were several, and so, when Paul and Barnabas got going, they will have made contact with the different synagogues.

MALCOLM

Would they be synagogues of different rites or doctrinal differences or just numerous synagogues all more or less the same?

ALEC

I don't think they'd be for different national groups, as was the case in Jerusalem. They would be rather like the numerous churches that we have in one city today where there's a large population.

MALCOLM

Then there were also a lot of Christians here. They came, I suppose, after the persecutions in Jerusalem that followed the stoning of Stephen.

7. Acts 13: 5.

ALEC

That's right. Acts tells us that Christians had made their way to Cyprus.[8] Thus in the synagogues here there were both orthodox Jews and Jewish Christians, and they seem to have got on well together. They were all Jews. There were no Gentile converts here yet.

MALCOLM

What puzzles me, Alec, is what these early Christians really believed – what held them together. It's an obvious fact but I must admit that it didn't dawn on me immediately: they hadn't got the Gospels.

ALEC

No; their Bible was what we call the Old Testament, which they were constantly reading in order to see how all the prophecies had been pointing forward to the coming of Jesus and were fulfilled in him.

MALCOLM

But, apart from that, they hadn't a single written word?

ALEC

Maybe not actually written down, but they had a very simple and definite sort of creed. 'Jesus is Lord' was the first Christian creed or confession,[9] and one could say that it was pregnant with all the further development of the faith.

MALCOLM

But, Alec, I find it difficult to understand. How could the Christians be on really good terms with the synagogues when

8. Acts 11:19.
9. 1 Corinthians 12:3.

they were believing and preaching something that was completely opposed to the views of those in the synagogue? Namely, that the Messiah had come and was not to be awaited. He had been put to death by the machinations of the high priest and so on.

ALEC

Yes, but belief in the Messiah was not the essential mark of Judaism. It was the Torah, the Law, that was the essential bond of all Jews; that is what held them together, however much they might differ in other matters, including how the Torah was to be interpreted. The Christians at this early stage were like a group or a sect within Judaism which happened to hold the belief that Jesus was the Messiah. There were many other different groups in Judaism in addition to the Pharisees and the Sadducees. There were, for instance, the Essenes and the Zealots. The Christians appeared to be another such group. That was the present state of affairs.

MALCOLM

And of course what they believed hadn't yet been formulated. I mean, if a man said that he wanted to be a Christian, you couldn't say to him, Here are the Thirty-Nine Articles, or whatever it might be.

ALEC

No, certainly not Thirty-Nine Articles! or anything as elaborate or complicated as that. But just look at what Paul says in one of his letters about the teaching which he received before he passed it on to his converts. That is to say, what had been formulated before he became a Christian. This is pretty definite and it's confirmed by what is said elsewhere in the

New Testament. This is what Paul says in 1 Corinthians 15:
3-5.

> ... *I delivered to you as of first importance what I also received,*
> *that Christ died for our sins in accordance with the scriptures,*
> *that he was buried, that he was raised on the third day in ac-*
> *cordance with the scriptures, and that he appeared to Cephas,*
> *then to the twelve. ...*

That is definite enough, isn't it, Malcolm?

MALCOLM

Oh, yes. But, granting that, I'm surely right in thinking that
they had no liturgy, no priesthood, no dogma, no scriptures?

ALEC

Wait a minute. They had the Jewish synagogue service which
was thoroughly liturgical, and in their own meetings, which
were at this time held in private houses, they read extracts
from the Old Testament scriptures which were specially
seen to be fulfilled in Jesus. And then they had the rites of
baptism and the Lord's Supper which were then, as they
have been ever since, of central importance. So altogether
the apostles had plenty to preach about and plenty of teaching
to give. All this was taking shape, though it was in a fluid or
flexible form during the first hundred years or so of Christian
history.

MALCOLM

At all events, here in Salamis Paul was able to speak in the
synagogues, to worship with his fellow Christians in their
homes, to partake of the Lord's Supper. And magically for
once – I think, I'm right in saying uniquely for once – it
caused no trouble.

ALEC

Trouble was to arise soon enough, but, as you say, so far things seemed to be going smoothly and happily.

At Aphrodite's Bay

MALCOLM

I can't imagine a more perfect scene than this exquisite sunlit bay, surrounded by these mighty rocks, as a site for the legendary birth of Aphrodite from the foam of the waves, nor indeed for Botticelli's marvellous picture of *The Birth of Venus*. I wonder whether Paul stopped here and what he thought about it.

ALEC

I doubt if he gave it a second thought, if he gave it one at all. More likely, he passed by with averted eyes on account of the associations of the place with pagan superstition. But that's no reason why we shouldn't stop here for a bit.

MALCOLM

I believe that in antiquity every island, town and city had its own favourite god or goddess, and here in Cyprus Aphrodite was the principal object of worship. I take it that they were all equally abhorrent to Paul.

ALEC

Yes, indeed. Anything connected with idolatry would have been horrifying to Paul and his companions.

MALCOLM

You mean because of the orthodox Jewish attitude to these
things?

ALEC

Exactly. The Second Commandment: 'You shall not make
yourself a graven image, or any likeness of anything that is in
heaven above, or that is in the earth beneath . . .'[10] This was
deeply ingrained in the Jewish mind.

MALCOLM

And I suppose that the debaucheries and the erotic aspect of
these pagan rites would have been particularly repellent to all
Jews.

ALEC

Certainly the things that went on at the pagan shrines, such
as temple prostitution, made the idolatry all the worse. They
were absolutely ruled out of consideration, and no Jew would
even look at these scenes, I guess.

MALCOLM

Did the Christians too in their preaching and teaching de-
nounce such things as the cult of Aphrodite?

ALEC

Every form of idolatry was as abhorrent to the early Christians as it was to the Jews. There may not be evidence in the
New Testament, except at Ephesus which of course we shall
come to later on, that they denounced particular idols, but
the whole thing was ruled out and terrible.

10. Exodus 20: 4.

MALCOLM

How far would you say that cults like this one of Aphrodite were flourishing at this time in the Roman Empire? Did people actually believe in them or were they just centres of excitement and interest?

ALEC

One must draw a distinction. The intellectuals, the philosophers, the sophists, and so on, mocked at them and didn't take them seriously, but they still had a hold on the people. And of course wherever you have shrines and idols and legends associated with them, there is very soon a financial interest in keeping them going. This consideration surely applied to all these cults.

MALCOLM

As may still be seen in many Christian cults today!

ALEC

And not only in Christian cults. It is true of other religions as well, and isn't it even the case that in Moscow there is a shrine in the Kremlin?

MALCOLM

What about the most horrible shrine of all, the Natural History Museum? People go there in great numbers.

ALEC

I don't know that that's quite parallel to what we were thinking about.

MALCOLM

Isn't science also a cult?

ALEC

I wouldn't call it that: no, it's quite a different matter and you're going off on a side track.

MALCOLM

Would you allow that going to see *Hair* or *Oh! Calcutta!* is parallel to the cult of Aphrodite?

ALEC

Ah! that may well be so: that is a much better analogy.

MALCOLM

Anyway, we agree that Paul and his companions hurried on to Paphos and didn't stop to admire the birthplace of Aphrodite.

At Paphos

MALCOLM

I see there are some ruins here of the Roman proconsul's residence, but much more attractive is the ancient basilica next door.

ALEC

They are evidently preparing to celebrate Easter . . . The very agreeable parish priest, with his long beard and chimney-pot hat and smattering of English, kindly says that we may sit in the stalls for our conversation here.

MALCOLM

You said that Paphos was at that time the capital of Cyprus, and that is why the proconsul, whose name was Sergius

Paulus, lived here. And Sergius Paulus, according to Acts, was greatly impressed by Paul and what he had to say.[11] Isn't he said to have become a believer? What does that signify?

ALEC

I'm rather doubtful whether it means that he became a baptized Christian, but obviously he was favourably impressed and well disposed.

MALCOLM

I have the feeling throughout Paul's letters and the Acts that he found it easier to deal with the Roman authorities – found himself instinctively more sympathetic with them – than with his fellow Hebrews and especially with the high priest and the authorities of Judaism.

ALEC

That does seem to be so. It has even been suggested that, if Acts is right about using his Roman name Paul instead of his Jewish name Saul from this time, he did this as a compliment to the governor Sergius Paulus.

MALCOLM

Some people might think that for a Jew, a Hebrew of the Hebrews as he calls himself, that was a somewhat unpatriotic attitude.

ALEC

On the other hand, the whole of his work as a missionary and the whole spread of the gospel depended on the *Pax Romana*, on the law and order which was maintained

11. Acts 13: 12.

throughout this part of the world by the Roman imperial authorities. For example, Paul was naturally very thankful to be able as a rule to travel about in safety. He had reason too to be grateful for his Roman citizenship.

MALCOLM

With Greek as the *lingua franca*?

ALEC

Yes, Greek was the common language of the Empire, and it was a great advantage to Paul to be able to make himself understood wherever he went.

MALCOLM

But he seems to go further than regarding these things as advantages. Doesn't he tell his fellow Christians that it is their duty to accept the authority that exists in the world and to obey it?

ALEC

Very true. His teaching about this was quite emphatic, as is plain from what he says in Chapter 13 of Romans:

> *Let every person be subject to the governing authorities. For there is no authority except from God, and those that exist have been instituted by God. Therefore he who resists the authorities resists what God has appointed, and those who resist will incur judgment.*

MALCOLM

This is a very unpalatable doctrine to many people today.

ALEC

It certainly is to all anarchists and would-be revolutionaries.

MALCOLM

And to other people also, among whom I could include myself – people who find the idea of earthly authority far from sympathetic and would find it extremely difficult to justify it in the terms Paul uses. But wasn't it perhaps the case that his attitude was based on the expectation that the whole thing would be shortly coming to an end and therefore there was no point in interfering with the Roman authority that prevailed? I mean, need it follow that he regarded the Roman authority as in itself admirable?

ALEC

He doesn't say 'admirable'. He regards it as providential that God has instituted civil government to maintain law and order. It's not the kingdom of God or anything like that.

MALCOLM

No, I shouldn't think so – in the days of the emperor Nero!

ALEC

It didn't matter so much who the emperor was. The whole system that maintained the *Pax Romana* was invaluable for the Christian mission.

MALCOLM

And from that Paul deduced a divine sanction of governing authority as such.

ALEC

He regarded it, I repeat, as providential that there was a system of law and order, and not anarchy or pure arbitrary despotism. I think that you, Malcolm, would be better pleased with Peter than with Paul in this matter, for, whereas Paul says, as we've seen, that civil government is divinely instituted, Peter is represented as saying that it is only a human institution,[12] though he is equally insistent that Christians should submit to it.

MALCOLM

I should certainly prefer to say that it is a human institution, but I'm not at all happy with so exclusive an emphasis on the duty of obedience to it.

ALEC

I readily admit that I should myself want to qualify what both Paul and Peter say about that.

MALCOLM

Anyway, it was here in Paphos that Paul established his first relations with the Roman authority, and they appear to have been very friendly and appreciative.

To Attalia

ALEC

Attalia, which is now called Antalya, was the sea port on the southern coast of Asia Minor (now Turkey). It was founded by Attalus II, who was king of Pergamum in the second century B.C., and was later annexed by the Roman Empire.

MALCOLM

Do you suppose that Paul and Barnabas stayed here?

12. I Peter 2:13.

ALEC

Apparently not on this occasion. There doesn't seem to have been a Jewish synagogue here, though there were many pagan cults. Paul came to Attalia only because it was the port that provided access to the city of Perga and the interior.

At Perga

MALCOLM

It is obvious from the ruins of Perga that it must have been an important and majestic city.

ALEC

But on this occasion they seem to have paid only a fleeting visit here too, though later they would come and preach here.[13] The only thing we're told that happened on this occasion was that John Mark left them.

MALCOLM

There was some sort of a row, I gather.

ALEC

The reason why he left isn't clear. Various guesses have been made. One is that he didn't at all like the idea of a journey up into the mountains, bandit-infested and dangerous as they were. Another is that he was simply a young man who was homesick and wanted to get back to Jerusalem where his mother lived or to Cyprus where he had relatives and friends. But a more likely reason is that at this time Mark's sympathies as regards the Christian mission were with Peter and the Jewish Christians in Jerusalem, rather than with Paul. That is

13. Acts 14:25.

70

to say, he was far from happy about the way in which he suspected – and rightly suspected – that Paul was going to welcome Gentiles into the Church. So he may be said to have parted on a matter of principle.

MALCOLM

Don't you think that people found it difficult to get on with Paul?

ALEC

No, I don't. He had an extraordinary power of gripping the affections and the faithfulness of his colleagues and associates both young and old. I regard this as a quite exceptional incident.

MALCOLM

But he was a very masterful person, wasn't he?

ALEC

Oh yes, and very impulsive. Personally, I think I would have found him rather difficult, but those who worked with him, apart from Mark, and of course Barnabas who afterwards parted over this same matter, got on well with him, so far as we know.

MALCOLM

I suppose it is possible that, just because Mark and Barnabas belonged to what one could call without irreverence the old gang, it was harder for them than for later comers to accept Paul's dominant leadership.

ALEC

That may very well be so.

71

MALCOLM

Anyway, he set out on this journey into the wild mountainous country to visit the cities beyond. Why do you think he did it?

ALEC

I am inclined to discount the theory that he had an attack of malaria here and wanted to get up into the high country.

MALCOLM

It's complete bosh, isn't it? I've had malaria myself, and I really know that that wouldn't be plausible.

ALEC

It is the case that Paul does say that he first preached to those cities in the interior because of an infirmity of the flesh.[14] But that leaves open the question what the infirmity was. Whatever it was, he was eager to get into the interior to cities where there were Roman colonies and a new sphere for their work.

MALCOLM

But he wasn't a robust person, was he?

ALEC

He must have been pretty tough to have coped with all the things he did and the journeys he made. But, from things he

14. Galatians 4:13.

---

7 '. . . but much more attractive is the ancient basilica . . .' (p. 65)
8 'I can't imagine a more perfect scene than this exquisite sunlit bay . . . as a site for the legendary birth of Aphrodite from the foam of the waves, nor indeed for Botticelli's marvellous picture of The Birth of Venus.' (p. 62)
9 'As they approached the island, they will have seen Salamis . . .' (p. 56)

says incidentally in his letters,[15] it is evident that he had some serious sort of physical trouble or disability. Nearly every kind of illness has been suggested. I myself think that most likely it was some nervous disorder that gave him splitting headaches and migraines and also affected his sight and his speech. This seems to account for most of the references to it.

MALCOLM

I suppose that in a case like this people always tend to credit the person in question with their own infirmities. I've always thought that he must have been an insomniac! But anyway reading his letters one can see quite clearly that he had the sort of temperament that today would be called manic-depressive. That is to say, his moods alternated violently. He'd be extremely cheerful and then very depressed. He could be extremely satirical and sharp, and at the same time very loving in his attitude to people. Don't you think this is true?

ALEC

Yes, I agree about that.

MALCOLM

Then what did he look like, Alec? That's what I should like to know.

ALEC

It's a natural question. While we've no absolutely authentic and reliable testimony, there is a passage I'd like to quote from a second-century book that as a whole is historically worthless, but this somehow seems to have the ring of authenticity. I wonder what you'll think of it.

15. 2 Corinthians 12:1–9; Galatians 4:13–15.

73

Paul, a man of small stature, with his eyebrows meeting and a rather large nose, somewhat baldheaded, bandylegged, strongly built, of gracious presence, for sometimes he looked like a man and sometimes he had the face of an angel.[16]

MALCOLM

I thought that was a terrific piece. Speaking as a writer, I would say quite categorically that it's almost sure to be true. You couldn't invent so vivid and lifelike a description, particularly that last bit.

Striking north from Perga

MALCOLM

I must say, Alec, travelling through these countries, especially these wild mountainous regions, I marvel continually how Paul managed to cover the enormous mileage that he did in his life-time.

ALEC

I couldn't agree more. Of course we don't really know how he travelled on land, whether on horseback or on foot, whether he hitchhiked or what. I can think of only one allusion to the way he travelled on land, namely when we are told that he went on horseback from Jerusalem to Caesarea.[17]

MALCOLM

That was under escort wasn't it?

16. 'The Acts of Paul and Thecla': see M. R. James, *The Apocryphal New Testament*, OUP (1924), p. 273.

17. Acts 23:24.

ALEC

That's right.

MALCOLM

But isn't there a reference somewhere to his going by carriage?

ALEC

Ah, that's good! You are thinking of the passage in Acts where it says, they took up their carriages and went on their journey.[18] But your trust in the Authorized Version, my dear Malcolm, lets you down there, because it doesn't mean that in the Greek. It means, they packed their bags and went on their way!

MALCOLM

I'm sure there are such mistakes in the Authorized Version but that doesn't alter my love for it.

ALEC

Nor mine.

MALCOLM

How do you think in point of fact Paul did travel for the most part? On foot?

ALEC

I suppose so, but we really don't know. It may be that historians of the hellenistic world have done recent work on means of travel at that time which I'm not familiar with. But I guess that he travelled in any way that was possible.

18. Acts 21:15.

Presumably, if there was a horse or a donkey available, he would be glad of it, or if he could get a lift in a chariot, he'd take it.

MALCOLM

The main roads were very crowded, weren't they? I've read about that: those great Roman roads, with all manner of people travelling on them, though there was no road of that kind running northward from Perga! What an amazing traveller Paul was! He seems to have had no home, no base, nowhere where his things were, nowhere to return to.

ALEC

No, not after his departure from Syrian Antioch.

MALCOLM

He really must have lived with his luggage, which I personally find even for a short time exceedingly uncomfortable.

ALEC

So do I, and our discomforts are surely trivial in comparison with those that Paul constantly took in his stride.

THE EVANGELIST

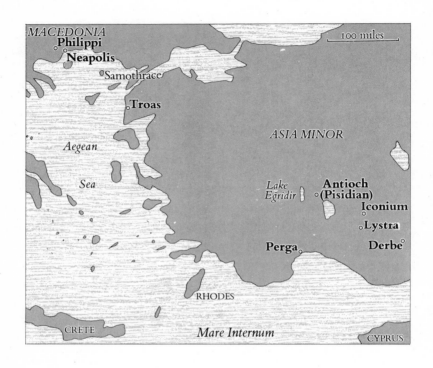

THE EVANGELIST

Introduction

ON their way from Perga to Antioch in Pisidia Paul and
Barnabas must have passed by Lake Eğridir which for sheer
beauty will stand comparison with any other lake in the
world. They still had a long and stiff journey ahead of them
before they reached their destination. When Paul delivered
his message in the synagogue at Pisidian Antioch, he had an
initial success. But the enthusiastic response that he received
aroused the jealousy of the Jewish officials who persuaded
the local magistrates to expel the missionaries from the city.
Henceforth Paul and Barnabas had no hesitation in seeking
Gentile converts. They travelled on to Iconium, Lystra and
Derbe, founding Christian communities in each place, but
also being followed up by persecuting Jews from Antioch
and so being compelled to move on. Eventually, they decided
to return to Syrian Antioch in order to report to the church
there on the outcome of their mission.

Before long, they were on the road again : at least Paul was.
It was at this point that Paul and Barnabas parted company
in consequence of a disagreement about whether or not
John Mark should go with them. Paul, who was now joined
by Silas and later by Timothy, first revisited the churches
that had already been founded and he was much encouraged
by the way in which they were devoloping. But his intention
was to go further afield, and as he went on his way he felt

himself being guided to go to Troas, whence it was easy to cross into Europe. Paul and his companions landed at Neapolis (now Kavalla) which was the port of Philippi in Macedonia. There Paul laid the foundations of what was to become one of his most attached and devoted Christian communities.

By Lake Eğridir

MALCOLM

I imagine that on their way to Antioch in Pisidia Paul and Barnabas must have paused to admire this absolutely marvellous lake.

ALEC

My dear Malcolm, when did Paul ever admire a view like this or indeed any natural scenery?

MALCOLM

I suppose you're right. You mean Paul wasn't a lover of nature.

ALEC

Quite so. His indifference to natural beauty derives partly from his Jewish background. There is very little appreciation of natural beauty for its own sake in the Old Testament. There are of course passages in the psalms about the heavens declaring the glory of God and so on, but on the whole the Jews were suspicious of the admiration of natural beauty because it was associated with paganism and idolatry.

80

MALCOLM

Do you think it was something that came in with Wordsworth?

ALEC

I wouldn't go as far as that, but nature mysticism, as we are
nowadays familiar with it, does largely derive, or at least
date, from him and the Lake poets.

MALCOLM

But this indifference to nature doesn't apply to Jesus himself,
does it? He used many most beautiful images taken from the
lake and from natural scenes of every kind.

ALEC

That is indeed very striking. Paul, on the other hand, took
his images from urban life.

MALCOLM

In a word, he was a townsman, and also rather a gregarious
man who enjoyed company. Apart from that time in the
Arabian desert, he never seems to have been alone. His
interest was in human beings, not in natural phenomena.

ALEC

Certainly.

MALCOLM

And his mysticism was centred not on nature but on God.

ALEC

Yes, and on Christ and on mankind as recreated in Christ.

MALCOLM

So as he walked by the shore of this beautiful lake, he will not have been preoccupied with it or with the mountains that surround it.

ALEC

I fear that is so. I regret it. To some extent it may be because he was short-sighted.

At Pisidian Antioch

MALCOLM

Then from the lake Paul and Barnabas journeyed on until they arrived at Antioch in Pisidia – not to be confused of course with the other Antioch, Syrian Antioch. There is hardly anything left now of Pisidian Antioch, just part of an aqueduct and a few ruins that have been excavated.

ALEC

True, but all the same there is more left of this than of many other towns and cities that were flourishing in Paul's time.

MALCOLM

Alec, one of the reasons I love travelling around this part of the world is that it reinforces my contempt for history. All this past obliterated, but not Paul's words.

ALEC

Surely you don't mean that you subscribe to Henry Ford's opinion that history is bunk.

MALCOLM

No, I wouldn't put it like that.

ALEC

I should hope not. For my part, I should prefer to say that all these ruins of antiquity remind me of Paul's words: 'The things that are seen are transient, but the things that are unseen are eternal.'[1]

MALCOLM

My God, we can agree on that. That is what I was trying to say. I think that what Paul meant by that saying of his is exactly what I meant.

ALEC

Well, in that case it would have been better if you had said that. It is not at all the same thing as saying that history is contemptible.

MALCOLM

Anyway, Paul and Barnabas arrived here in Antioch when it was still part of history. We can agree about that.

ALEC

Oh yes, it was a big and important city in those days.

MALCOLM

As usual, they made for the synagogue, where they could hope to find a ready-made audience.

1. 2 Corinthians 4: 18.

ALEC

When Paul went to the synagogue on their first Sabbath in the city, he was apparently recognized as something of a rabbi, presumably because he was wearing some of the badges that indicated that he was a Pharisee. So he was asked to give an address, and he made such a favourable impression that they asked him to speak again on the next Sabbath.

MALCOLM

The address that he gave on the first occasion, as one reads it in Acts started along perfectly orthodox Jewish lines, but of course it led up to a declaration of faith in Christ.

ALEC

The congregation, which no doubt included god-fearers[2] as well as Jews, seems to have been very much interested, with the result that on the following Sabbath there was a tremendous crowd. Acts says that 'almost the whole city' turned out to hear Paul.[3] However, the older Jews in the synagogue were evidently jealous of Paul's success in attracting many more hearers than they themselves could. So they took steps to stir up the local magistrates, who forced Paul and Barnabas to move on.

MALCOLM

Having been turned out of this city, they went on to other cities.

2. See p. 49 *supra*.
3. Acts 13 : 44.

At Iconium

ALEC

To Iconium in the first place. It no longer exists, but the large city of Konya is where it was. Here things seem to have gone very well for a time, and many Jews and Gentiles became Christian converts. But the orthodox Jews managed to start a commotion against the apostles, so that they were threatened with being stoned.

At Lystra

MALCOLM

So they went on to Lystra where they addressed themselves to Gentiles. Wasn't it at Lystra that Paul is said to have cured a lame man, which so excited the pagan inhabitants that they wanted to treat both him and Barnabas as gods – as Hermes and Zeus? That must have been utterly repugnant to them.

ALEC

Yes, indeed. But Paul and Barnabas, who weren't familiar with the local dialect, didn't at first realize what they were preparing to do. It was only when the priest of Zeus came out before his temple and prepared an altar that they grasped what was afoot, and were of course horrified at the intended idolatry.

MALCOLM

I love the words with which they repudiated any idea that men could be like gods and so be worshipped.

ALEC

This was Paul's first address to pagans that we have on record.

Men, why are you doing this? We also are men, of like nature with you, and bring you good news, that you should turn from these vain things to a living God who made the heaven and the earth and the sea and all that is in them. In past generations he allowed all the nations to walk in their own ways; yet he did not leave himself without witness, for he did good and gave you from heaven rains and fruitful seasons, satisfying your hearts with food and gladness.[4]

Acts adds that, 'With these words they scarcely restrained the people from offering sacrifice to them.' Before long Jews came through from Antioch and Iconium and caused the customary trouble, and so they went on to Derbe, where things seem to have gone more smoothly.

MALCOLM

One of the wonderful things about Paul's message is the way he drove home the truth that no man can ever be anything except just a mortal man, and that all he can ever hope to be or achieve or fulfil is through his relationship to God and that alone.

ALEC

We agree about that, if not about history!

At Syrian Antioch

MALCOLM

On their way back to their base at Syrian Antioch I suppose Paul and Barnabas were getting ready to make a sort of

4. Acts 14: 15–17.

report to the Christians there about their activities – about what they had been doing and how they had been getting on.

ALEC

They could look forward to making a very favourable report. After all, in spite of the opposition from Jews, they had suc-ceeded in founding a string of new churches in Galatia which had made a very promising start.

MALCOLM

What was it then that went wrong?

ALEC

Some time after they had got back to Syrian Antioch, news began to percolate through from the Galatian churches that emissaries from Jerusalem had been on Paul's tracks there. These Jewish Christians, or judaizers as they may be called, had been disturbing the converts in Galatia, running down Paul as a bogus apostle, and telling the people there that he had given them a false idea of what being a Christian meant. And it was this that provoked him to write the first of his letters that have survived, namely the so-called Epistle to the Galatians.[5]

MALCOLM

When Paul wanted to send a message to one of his churches, there was sure to be some young man around who would take it down from Paul's dictation. It might well be one of

5. There is a difference of opinion among scholars about whether this epistle was addressed to the churches in southern Galatia (Antioch in Pisidia, etc.) or to churches in northern Galatia of the foundation of which Acts contains no clear record. The former opinion is here preferred.

the people we are told about, such as Timothy or Silas. He would have a piece of papyrus in front of him, and then Paul would sit down and dictate as you or I might.

ALEC

The fact that this is how Paul wrote his letters explains why they are sometimes difficult to understand, and why their style is often jerky. They were not carefully prepared and polished literary compositions, nor of course had he any idea that they would be read for centuries to come and, as it were, be canonized. At the end of a letter which he had dictated, Paul would often take the pen into his own hand and write a few additional sentences, as he does in Galatians.[6] 'See', he says, 'with what large letters I am writing to you with my own hand.'

MALCOLM

He may have written in these large letters because he was having trouble with his eyesight. Short-sighted people tend to have large handwriting.

ALEC

Anyhow, that is more or less how Paul wrote his letters. Another interesting question about them is how they came

6. Galatians 6: 11.

10 '. . . he somehow felt moved by the Spirit to go to Troas, which was near the ancient city of Troy.' (p. 93)
11 'Then from the lake Paul and Barnabas journeyed on until they arrived at Antioch in Pisidia.' (p. 82)
12 'We are walking along the very road from Neapolis to Philippi that Paul took.' (p. 97)

to be collected. The probable answer is that about the end of the first century some enterprising Christian went round the various churches that Paul had founded and corresponded with, and asked the Christians whether – in their archives or strongbox or whatever they had – they had preserved any letters from Paul. Where he found any, he got permission to copy them out, and so was able to make a collection of them.

MALCOLM

Well now, what about Galatians?

ALEC

As soon as you begin to read this letter it is evident that Paul was having to defend the genuineness of his own apostleship against the judaizing people who had been running him down and saying he was no real apostle. They alleged that he picked up his message from the original apostles, and in doing so had distorted and watered it down, and so had misled those who had been taken in by him. Thus in the first part of Galatians Paul was asserting, with the utmost conviction and emphasis, that he was as real an apostle as any of the others, that he had been directly appointed by God, and that he had received his gospel directly from God and not from any men whatever.

MALCOLM

So he spoke with authority, his own authority, as distinct from the judaic authority of the scribes that he had recognized when he was a Pharisee.

ALEC

Yes, exactly. One or two short quotations from the letter will bring this out.

89

O foolish Galatians! Who has bewitched you, before whose eyes Jesus Christ was publicly portrayed as crucified? Let me ask you only this: Did you receive the Spirit by works of the law, or by hearing with faith?[7]

He means that he had told them that they got right with God by putting their whole trust in Christ crucified and that they didn't have to depend for their justification on doing all the works of the Law.

MALCOLM

That surely was the essence of the whole matter – the contrast between faith and law.

ALEC

Yes, Paul kept on driving the point home. 'For freedom', he writes, 'Christ has set us free; stand fast therefore, and do not submit again to a yoke of slavery. [That is, the slavery of having to obey all the precepts of the Law, which Paul's judaizing opponents were trying to impose on them.] Now I, Paul, say to you that if you receive circumcision, Christ will be of no advantage to you.'[8]

MALCOLM

I suppose that circumcision was a kind of outward and visible manifestation of an inward and invisible adherence to a whole body of law. Is that right?

ALEC

Yes. 'The Circumcision' was one of the names – a sort of nickname – for Judaism. Just as the Baptists are so called

7. Galatians 3: 1 f.
8. Galatians 5: 1 f.

because they practise adult or believer's baptism, although there is much more to their faith and practice than that, so Judaism was called 'the Circumcision', although there was much more to it than that. Circumcision figured prominently and was a matter of contention, because it was the most difficult thing for a Gentile, who was attracted to Judaism, to accept. For adult men it involved a painful operation. Then it was mocked at by non-Jews. Moreover, it was a thing that couldn't be kept secret since in those days, when men went to the public baths, they went naked.

MALCOLM

Anyway, the question of circumcision became a sort of crystallization of this row. Paul's opponents said that in order to become a Christian a man must be circumcised and accept all the obligations that went with it. And Paul said, No. Now, as regards the Law, it seems to me that in men's minds there always exists the illusion that they can find a basis for living in a law – in the case of the Jews, in propositions which they believed had been revealed to them by God. Paul's gospel was one of liberation because he declared that what really mattered was not obedience to any law but faith in Christ.

ALEC

Yes, that's right. I would put it like this. All men are enslaved, some to law and some to absence of law, and Christ liberates all men, whatever the slavery in which they are involved. One can be enslaved to one's own passions, or to conventional standards of conduct, or to the American way of life, etc.

MALCOLM

Or take the idea of progress, that's a law isn't it, which in our time has imprisoned men utterly?

91

ALEC

I don't follow you there; it seems to me a rather far-fetched idea that would need a lot of elaborating. I regard the idea of progress as highly ambiguous and in many respects illusory, but I wouldn't call it a law in this context.

MALCOLM

I would, because I think it is something that enslaves men. I mean the belief that through the notion of progress they can live satisfactorily in terms of this world alone. But, however that may be, the Law, as Paul saw it, was quite specifically the Law of Judaism, the Torah, handed down as they believed by God.

ALEC

The heart of Paul's message comes out in this great passage in Galatians:

> . . . *if you are led by the Spirit you are not under the law. Now the works of the flesh are plain: immorality, impurity, licentiousness, idolatry, sorcery, enmity, strife, jealousy, anger, selfishness, dissension, party spirit, envy, drunkenness, carousing, and the like.* [All those things are included in what Paul means by 'the flesh'.] *I warn you* [he continues], *as I warned you before, that those who do such things shall not inherit the kingdom of God. But the fruit of the Spirit is love, joy, peace, patience, kindness, goodness, faithfulness, gentleness, self-control . . .* [9]

MALCOLM

Exactly. So this man indomitably, fearlessly, tirelessly went travelling about the world, to tell people this truth that he had learned and that had changed the whole course of his life.

9. Galatians 5: 18–23.

On the road again

ALEC
He must have travelled thousands and thousands of miles.

MALCOLM
And, as I imagine, getting into conversation with people and always in the end coming back to this point, his truth.

ALEC
Yes, he won't of course have gone round asking people 'Are you saved?', but he will certainly have been alive to every opportunity of telling them about Christ and the new life in the Spirit.

MALCOLM
And making his light shine. I can't help feeling too that this perpetual motion in Paul's life somehow suited his temperament.

ALEC
Anyway, soon after they got back to Syrian Antioch and had made their report, Paul was off again on another journey. This time instead of Barnabas he took Silas with him. First, they went through the Galatian churches, and he meant to go on and evangelize other parts of Asia Minor. But as they went on he somehow felt moved by the Spirit to go to Troas, which was near the ancient city of Troy.

At Troas

MALCOLM

Do you think Paul was really moved by the Spirit to come here? Or was it something that was put in afterwards by the author of Acts to explain what happened?

ALEC

All that we have about this is the record in Acts which presents it as guidance by the Spirit. Whether you consider that it actually was so or not depends on whether you believe in the Holy Spirit.

MALCOLM

Yes, of course. Anyhow, the simple fact is that he did come to Troas with his companions, and subsequently they went on together to what was then Macedonia.

ALEC

What led to their next move was a curious incident that occurred while Paul was at Troas. One night he had a dream or vision of a man of Macedonia standing by him and saying, 'Come over and help us'.[10] Some people have thought that this was Luke (he may have been a native of Philippi) who had come over and was actually standing by Paul's bed. Whether it was Luke or a dream or a vision, what is certain is that Paul decided to act upon it.

MALCOLM

And his acting upon it was without any exaggeration one of the very decisive moments in history.

10. Acts 16: 9.

ALEC

Unquestionably: it meant that the Christian faith was for the first time brought into what we now call Europe.

MALCOLM

How extraordinary, how fantastic, it is to reflect that Paul came to this place where we now are and took a decision whereby two thousand years of Christendom, of our civilization, of our history, all came to pass.

ALEC

I like the way the story of Paul's departure from Troas is rounded off in Acts:

> . . . when he had seen the vision, immediately we sought to go on into Macedonia, concluding that God had called us to preach the gospel to them.[11]

MALCOLM

And so they sailed across to what is now northern Greece, carrying the gospel to Europe.

At Neapolis

MALCOLM

It was at this little port that Paul first landed in Europe. I don't suppose that he had much baggage with him, but he was carrying a great light to shine in the darkness of a sick world. He was taking with him a new faith, a new hope, a new freedom. Do you think, Alec, that he had any idea of how momentous an occasion this was?

11. Acts 16: 10.

95

ALEC

That's difficult to say. But Paul and his companions would be in a happy frame of mind on a lower level than you're speaking about, because they had had a jolly good voyage. Whereas later we are told that this voyage took five days, on this occasion they got through in two days, stopping only at Samothrace, the island that goes up to five thousand feet and is a great landmark.[12] A good voyage makes a favourable start to a new enterprise, wouldn't you say?

MALCOLM

And what an enterprise it was – the conversion of the civilized world! This was his point of departure for all the great cities of the West and ultimately for Rome, the then capital of the world. It is difficult to visualize the scene, because Paul no doubt looked just a very obscure passenger among all the others.

ALEC

And of course he could not know how things were going to develop, but we can be sure that he was full of hope and expectation.

MALCOLM

It is difficult also to think of any comparable arrival. Perhaps, on an infinitely lower scale, Lenin arriving unknown at the Finland Station in Petrograd in 1917. At the time nobody could have guessed what would come of that. Paul's arrival touched off two thousand years of history, the story of Christendom with all its fantastic and sublime achievements and all its wickedness and terror. And now one feels that the

12. Acts 16: 11; 20: 6.

impetus is spent. The light has gone out, and what we need is
another man to land in another port, and make it shine again.

On the Via Egnatia

MALCOLM

We are walking along the very road from Neapolis to Philippi
that Paul took.

ALEC

It is known as the Via Egnatia or the Egnatian Way.[13] It
started at Neapolis and went right through to what is now
Durazzo on the Adriatic, and so to Rome. It was one of the
great trunk-roads of the time.

MALCOLM

It is a most extraordinary thing to think that we are here
treading on the self-same stones that Paul trod. Nothing I'm
sure could have been more natural than for Paul to make for
Philippi.

ALEC

It's the first place they would come to. It's about nine miles
inland from the port.

MALCOLM

And it led to the great cities of Macedonia that Paul was so
eager to visit.

13. The Via Egnatia was so called after a town of that name in southern
Italy which was situated on one of the great Roman roads.

At Philippi

ALEC

Philippi itself wasn't perhaps a great city, though it was quite an important place. It was a Roman colony. It is natural that Paul should have paused here, even if he wasn't expecting to stay long.

MALCOLM

Would there already be any Christians at Philippi?

ALEC

Probably not.

MALCOLM

But he did meet such Jews as there were – at a little stream near the town. How did that come about?

ALEC

It would appear that there weren't enough Jews at Philippi for there to be a synagogue. And when Jews had no synagogue, they repaired for their devotions and ablutions on the Sabbath to running water, and at Philippi the river Gangites flowed just outside the walls.

MALCOLM

And there he encountered a lady by the name of Lydia, didn't he?

ALEC

Apparently she was the widow of a prosperous businessman from Thyatira who sold purple garments. She became a convert and her whole household was baptized, and they invited Paul and his companions to stay with them.

MALCOLM

Then inevitably trouble arose.

ALEC

It was rather complicated trouble on this occasion. Some people, with whose financial interests Paul had interfered, appealed to the magistrates, alleging that he was causing disobedience to the decrees of Caesar and that he was a very disturbing influence. In the end the magistrates asked Paul and his companions to go on.

MALCOLM

After they'd been imprisoned?

ALEC

According to the story in Acts they had a night in prison.

MALCOLM

But wasn't there a mysterious episode arising from a thunderstorm or something?

ALEC

It was an earthquake according to Acts, but I think that was probably a tall story that got inserted in the record. It makes perfectly good sense without that.

MALCOLM

So the same pattern repeats itself. He talks to the people; they are fascinated by what he says; they respond to it until they see what he is really driving at, and then they turn against him and persecute him, and there is nothing for it but for him to go on elsewhere.

ALEC

It is almost like an illustration of the saying that 'nothing fails like success'. After initial success there was an apparent failure.

MALCOLM

Failure! I suppose that in all history no man has ever embarked upon a mission that has been so staggeringly successful.

ALEC

Ah, yes, in the final reckoning.

THE MISSIONARY

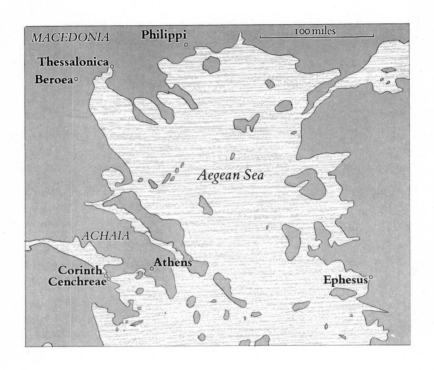

THE MISSIONARY

Introduction

FROM Philippi Paul and his two companions, Silas and Timothy, went along the coast road to Thessalonica (Salonika). A Christian community was founded there, to which later on Paul was to address the two letters known as 1 and 2 Thessalonians. He had to cut short his first visit because the orthodox Jews, who were jealous of the success of the Christian missionaries, roused the rabble against them and they had to move on.[1]

They now made for the city of Beroea (Verria) which was about fifty miles inland. Here they received an even more encouraging welcome and made many notable converts among both Jews and Gentiles. It was not until some of the Jews, who had been hostile to Paul at Thessalonica, arrived on the scene and renewed their attacks on him that the Christians pressed him to depart in the interests of his own safety. But Silas and Timothy stayed on for a time to guide this young church in its early days.[2]

Meanwhile Paul reached Athens. He was appalled by the evidences of idolatry which he saw all around him, and he couldn't refrain from giving the Athenians, who congregated in the market-place, a piece of his mind. On a famous occasion he addressed a group of philosophers on Mars' hill, though without much success. He wanted to get on to Corinth which was a more promising field for missionary work. Here one of

1. Acts 17:1–9.   2. Acts 17: 10–14.

the liveliest of the Pauline churches came into being, and the apostle stayed longer than he had done elsewhere.[3]

However, as soon as he felt free to go on, he sailed from Cenchreae, which was one of the ports of Corinth, for Ephesus. After a round of brief visits to Syrian Antioch and the Galatian churches, Paul decided to settle at Ephesus for a considerable time. Eventually he made so many converts that the commercial interests, which catered for the cult of the goddess Diana, found that their livelihood was being threatened, and so they engineered a demonstration against the Christians which culminated in a wild gathering in the theatre. Although Paul wasn't directly involved in this affray, it seemed advisable that he should make himself scarce for some time and so he went off to revisit the Macedonian churches.[4]

At Thessalonica

ALEC

I think it's quite likely that Paul, Silas and Timothy did this part of their journey – from Philippi to Thessalonica – on horseback, because the places where Acts says they stopped on the way are far enough apart for a comfortable day's riding but too far apart for walking.

3. Acts 17: 16–18:18. 4. Acts 18: 18–20:1.

---

13 '. . . the great temple of Athene, the Parthenon, which was behind Paul as he spoke . . .' (p. 112)

14 'My dear Malcolm, when did Paul ever admire a view like this or indeed any natural scenery?' (p. 80)

15 'As he approached the city he will have had in view the great hill behind, known as the Acrocorinthus.' (p. 114)

MALCOLM

I understand that Thessalonica was a much more important place than Philippi, in fact a very large city, as it is today, although practically nothing of Paul's Thessalonica remains now. Many British people know about Salonika because of the part it played in the two world wars.

ALEC

There was a considerable colony of Jews here and of course a synagogue, so Paul was able to get to work at once, teaching and preaching, and to start with he had very heartening results.

MALCOLM

And then another row. It's the same essential pattern that seems to repeat itself in all these places.

ALEC

Only the details vary. On this occasion the orthodox Jews, jealous of Paul's success, roused the rabble against him and his companions and brought them before the city authorities, alleging that 'these men who had been turning the world upside down'[5] were promoting sedition by proclaiming a rival king to Caesar. Paul, it seems, had been preaching about the kingdom of God and they had wilfully misunderstood what he was saying.

MALCOLM

When they spoke about turning the world upside down, they spoke more truly than they knew!

5. Acts 17: 6.

ALEC

Yes, indeed. It is interesting that after this time Paul apparently dropped using the expression 'the kingdom of God' so as to give no pretext for the kind of misunderstanding that was exploited here.

MALCOLM

Yet despite these troubles a very substantial church was established at Thessalonica.

ALEC

We can infer that from Paul's letters to the Thessalonian Christians. In one of them he wrote: 'You became an example to all the believers in Macedonia and in Achaia. For not only has the word of the Lord sounded forth from you in Macedonia and Achaia, but your faith in God has gone forth everywhere.'[6] There's another striking thing about these letters. They show how agitated some of the Thessalonians were about the teaching they'd received that Christ's return in glory was imminent.

MALCOLM

You mean they were taught that the end of the world was coming quite soon?

ALEC

Exactly. 'The end of all things is at hand',[7] is a New Testament saying, though not Paul's. But that sounds rather negative, whereas their expectation was a positive one. The emphasis was on the final appearing of Christ and his bringing all things to fulfilment. Evidently some of the Thessalonians were so preoccupied with this expectation, which indeed they'd been

6. I Thessalonians I: 7 f.
7. I Peter 4: 7.

told to look and hope for, that they could hardly think of anything else. If everything was coming to an end quite soon, what need was there, for instance, to work?

MALCOLM

I can see their point. And, you know, this is one of the things that to the modern mind is a great stumbling block. People are liable to say – I'm sure it's been said to you as it has been to me – that these early Christians firmly believed the world was coming to an end, and that all their beliefs and hopes were bound up with that. Well, they say, the world didn't come to an end, and that really invalidates the whole thing.

ALEC

It's a plausible objection, but I wouldn't at all allow that it's a valid objection to the Christian faith. At first sight it does appear to have been an illusory expectation. But on a pro-founder view it is a vivid way of expressing a permanent truth. For time is always about to be cut off by eternity both for the individual and for the race. All things are always coming to an end both in the sense of coming to their conclusion and also of coming to their fulfilment. The early Christians, by taking this expectation literally – by supposing that the end of all things and the final appearing of Christ were, so to speak, just around the corner – have engrained this expectation in the Christian imagination as it wouldn't have been in any other way, and that is very salutary for us all. It has made Christians aware, and should always keep them aware, that 'here we have no lasting city, but we seek the city which is to come'.[8]

MALCOLM

I can see that it is a sovereign antidote to all forms of utopian-ism and secularism, including 'secular Christianity'.

8. Hebrews 13: 14.

ALEC

It has been said that the true Christian feels himself to be living between the lightning of Christ's first coming and the thunder of his final appearing. It also reminds me of that saying of Dr Johnson how being under sentence of death marvellously clears or concentrates a man's mind. The fact that the early Christians thought that everything was under sentence of death, and of fulfilment beyond that, enabled them to see temporal and eternal values in their right proportions. In consequence, we've got this perspective – this outlook on the present world – enshrined for ever in the New Testament.

MALCOLM

Still, it must have been difficult for Paul to deal with the situation at Thessalonica. He'd got to uphold what he believed to be the case, and at the same time to check the tendency of the more emotional of his converts to say, 'Well, if the world's coming to an end, what does it matter what I do?' They could say this all the more readily because of Paul's apparent depreciation of the works of the Law.

ALEC

You are right. Some of Paul's critics accused him of demoralizing his converts and of so exciting them with fervent expectations that they became indifferent to the duties of everyday life.[9] Have you noticed too how Paul and other New Testament writers constantly had to tell their converts to be sober and to think soberly?[10] That must have been

9. Romans 3: 8.

10. Romans 12:3; 1 Thessalonians 5:6,8; Titus 2:2, 12; 1 Peter 1:13; 4:7;5:8.

because they were liable to become over-excited. While it was true that the end of all things would come in God's good time and they were to live as pilgrims, not as permanent residents, on earth, they were not all the time to be agitating themselves about the end.

At Beroea

MALCOLM

Paul's next objective was Beroea, a city beautifully situated up in hilly country. Extraordinary man! Every time he is pushed out of one place, he picks himself up and goes on to the next. And in the next he's received with what seems to me surprising enthusiasm, when one considers the reputation that would supposedly have preceded him. It occurs to me that he can't have been as well known as we are inclined to imagine. If he had been, information about him and the disturbing effects of his visits would have preceded him and he would have been received with some reserve and suspicion when he presented himself in the synagogue.

ALEC

Yes, I'm sure we tend to have an exaggerated idea of how well known Paul was in his life-time.

MALCOLM

Beroea is unique among the places we have so far been to, for here we actually have before our eyes the old Jewish quarter of the city and a very ancient synagogue. The present building may not date from Paul's time, but it undoubtedly is on the same site and some of the stones in this one were probably in the one where he first spoke to the people of Beroea.

ALEC

As usual things seem to have gone very well here to begin with and for quite a time. Acts gives the Beroean converts high marks:

> These Jews were more noble than those in Thessalonica, for they received the word with all eagerness, examining the scriptures daily to see if these things were so. Many of them therefore believed, with not a few Greek women of high standing as well as men.[11]

But, also as usual, trouble started in due course. The orthodox Jews from Thessalonica got wind of what was happening here and followed Paul up.

MALCOLM

Why did they have such a mania to persecute him?

ALEC

I suppose they realized that the Christian teaching and preaching threatened the whole Jewish system based on the Torah. Paul's preaching really put a bomb under it.

MALCOLM

So all his efforts to present himself as a Pharisee, as a strict Jew, were of no avail so soon as he broached the subject of the Christian revelation. Now after the row in Beroea he went on to Athens, didn't he?

ALEC

Yes, he left Silas and Timothy here to superintend matters. Some of the Beroean Christians saw him on his way – ac-

11. Acts 17: 11 f.

cording to Acts[12] – 'to the sea'. I don't think that means that he went by sea, but that he went by the coast road.

At Athens (Mars' hill)

MALCOLM
Paul's intention seems to have been to wait quietly in Athens until Silas and Timothy were able to join him. But when he saw all the evidences of idolatry and felt the general atmosphere of the place, he couldn't contain himself, and he was soon preaching and telling people, first in the synagogue and then in the agora or market-place, about Jesus and the Christian gospel. As regards the general atmosphere of the place Acts says that 'all the Athenians and the foreigners who lived there spent their time in nothing except telling or hearing something new'.[13] That's very much like today, I should say.

ALEC
There were plenty of people in those days travelling around the Roman Empire, peddling new ideas.

MALCOLM
Like the maharishis!

ALEC
They would all come to Athens sooner or later.

MALCOLM
So the eggheads, the intellectuals, the Stoic and Epicurean philosophers, heard about Paul and invited him to address them here on Mars' hill.

12. Acts 17: 14.   13. Acts 17: 21.

ALEC

We can stand today on the actual spot where Paul did speak to them. The words that he addressed to these sages, as given in Acts, are very interesting and different, I would say, from any other address of his that is on record.

> *So Paul, standing in the middle of Mars' hill, said: 'Men of Athens, I perceive that in every way you are very religious. For as I passed along, and observed the objects of your worship, I found also an altar with this inscription, "To an unknown god". What therefore you worship as unknown, this I proclaim to you. The God who made the world and everything in it, being Lord of heaven and earth, does not live in shrines made by man, nor is he served by human hands, as though he needed anything, since he himself gives to all men life and breath and everything. . . .*
>
> *'The times of ignorance God overlooked, but now he commands all men everywhere to repent, because he has fixed a day on which he will judge the world in righteousness by a man whom he has appointed, and of this he has given assurance to all men by raising him from the dead.'*[14]

Of course the great temple of Athene, the Parthenon, which was behind Paul as he spoke, must have underlined his words.

MALCOLM

Alec, what impression do you think this speech made on these people?

ALEC

Not much of an impression, I should say. The early part consisted of the commonplaces of Stoic philosophy, which

14. Acts 17: 22 – 5, 30 f.

was of course a skilful way of approaching this audience, but when he turned round and spoke about the coming judgment, in terms that were reminiscent of Jewish apocalyptic, and above all when he spoke of the resurrection, they will have thought it was nonsense. Acts gives the impression that Paul made only a handful of converts here, not enough to make him want to stay and try to build up a church here.

At Athens (the Acropolis)

MALCOLM

Paul must have walked up here, to this great temple of Athene, during his stay in Athens, mustn't he?

ALEC

I wonder. I fancy he spent most of his time down in the market-place. If he did come up here, he won't have felt much appreciation of the architecture or the statuary. Phidias left him cold.

MALCOLM

Nor would he have appreciated the magnificent situation of the Acropolis. How do you think he passed his days when he was in Athens?

ALEC

It would be very interesting if we could describe a specimen day of his. We have no precise evidence, but we can be pretty sure that he spent a lot of time talking to people and also a good deal of time in prayer both by himself and with his fellow Christians.

MALCOLM

One thing I am quite certain about is that sight-seeing didn't play any part in his life! What a fantastic thing sight-seeing has become in the twentieth century! Almost like a religion. People endlessly processing through places like the Acropolis. The stones worn down like the steps of the Scala Sancta in Rome where people go up on their knees. The endless recitation and intonation of liturgies by the guides, in innumerable languages, as the facts are given to the pilgrims as they pass through, and then the monetary offering at the gate! It's the religion of modern man. After all, where could you find more of a holy of holies than the American Express office in any city? There the worshippers throng.

At Corinth

MALCOLM

After his somewhat disappointing experience in Athens, Paul went on to Corinth.

ALEC

As he approached the city he will have had in view the great hill behind it, known as the Acrocorinthus, on which the acropolis is situated, and no doubt he was wondering what sort of a reception he would get here.

MALCOLM

It was in fact a large cosmopolitan city with a bad name for dissolute behaviour, wasn't it?

ALEC

It certainly was. The Greek word *korinthiazesthai* meant to fornicate. It was notorious for its immorality. It was a sort of Vanity Fair of the ancient world. Paul made many more

converts here than in Athens. Although after a time he had to
break with the synagogue, he was able to build up a large
congregation, consisting mainly of Gentiles.

MALCOLM

Didn't the Jews at some point try to involve Roman authority
against Paul?

ALEC

Yes, after about eighteen months they brought charges
against him before the Roman proconsul whose name was
Gallio.

MALCOLM

I understand that he provides one of the few hard dates in the
story.

ALEC

True: it fixes Paul's time at Corinth in the early fifties A.D.,
when Paul himself was probably in his early fifties. Exactly
what the charges were that were brought against Paul is
obscure, but anyhow the case was dismissed by the proconsul.

MALCOLM

Still, one can easily imagine the scene, for Gallio's judgment seat has been excavated. A large crowd presumably
assembled, public interest was aroused, and the Jews would be
there to bring their case, and Paul to defend himself.

ALEC

The fact that the proconsul dismissed the case turned to Paul's
advantage. It cleared Paul and the Christians from any
suspicion of being condemned by Rome.

MALCOLM

After this affair Paul stayed on in Corinth for some time, but as soon as he was satisfied that the Corinthian Christians could manage without him he wanted to revisit the churches he had previously founded and then to break new ground. So he set sail from Cenchreae, one of the ports of Corinth, a beautifully situated little harbour which has recently been excavated.

At Cenchreae

ALEC

There is plenty of evidence that Paul continued to take a lively interest in the Corinthian church. That is shown both by the subsequent visits he paid to it and still more by the letters he wrote. We know of at least four letters that he wrote to the Corinthian Christians. Fragments of two which have disappeared as a whole are to be found in what we call 2 Corinthians.

MALCOLM

But 1 Corinthians is more or less as he wrote it?

ALEC

Surely; and it deals with a number of very important subjects. There's a whole chapter, for instance, about questions relating to marriage. Lots of people seem to imagine that Paul had a very low view of marriage and even that he was a woman-hater. Well, that is nonsense at any rate. He had many women friends and associates.

MALCOLM

Including one who sailed with him from here.

ALEC

Yes, Priscilla. The messages that he sends to his women friends in his letters are obvious evidence of his happy relations with them. As regards marriage, Paul wasn't sentimental or romantic about it, but down to earth and commonsensical. Some of the things he said were no doubt conditioned by the fact that he thought the world was soon coming to an end. So he has nothing much to say about the importance of bringing up a family. Also like everyone else at that time he took it for granted that in the family the wife was subordinate to the husband. But I can't see that there is anything wrong with his oft quoted saying that it is better to marry than to burn.[15] If it is seen in its context, it is elementary good sense. He is saying to people who are separated from their spouses or divorced or unmarried or would-be celibates, that if they are aflame with sensual desire, it is far better for them to marry than to go on like that. I should have thought that is the right advice to give to anyone in that position. I'm a celibate myself and if anyone had given this advice to me, I should have thought it very sensible, though happily I didn't need to take it!

MALCOLM

I suppose the best thing of all in 1 Corinthians is the famous Chapter 13 which I'm sure we would both agree is one of the most enchanting and wonderful things ever written. The chapter which begins: 'Though I speak with the tongues of men and of angels, and have not charity [or love], I am become as sounding brass, or a tinkling cymbal.' Unfortunately both the words 'charity' and 'love' have been debased in modern speech, but Paul is talking about something that transcends every sort of human endeavour but which none-

15. 1 Corinthians 7: 9.

theless is essential if any human endeavour is to be worthwhile.

ALEC

Yes, the kind of love Paul was writing about is love for the
unlovely and unlovable, love that seeks nothing for itself, in
fact the love which is divine.

MALCOLM

I would say that this was Paul's sublimest utterance. I don't
think he ever touched a higher point than this.

ALEC

I can't believe he just dictated it on the spur of the moment.
He must have worked on it for a long time. It has been well
said that he didn't think it up but copied it down; that is to
say, he was really copying down what he'd seen in his vision
of Christ.

In the streets of Ephesus

MALCOLM

From Cenchreae Paul sailed to Ephesus. Its extensive ruins –
finer than any others that we have seen – make it possible to
picture what a great hellenistic city was like. In Paul's time,
Ephesus as well as being an important centre of commerce
had a large harbour which is now silted up. We can be sure
Paul walked along these streets and perhaps made purchases
at these shops, for that is evidently what they were.

ALEC

There was a biggish Jewish community here. But Paul paid
only a flying visit to Ephesus in the first instance. Before settling here, he made a rapid tour to see how the Christians at

Syrian Antioch and in the Galatian churches were getting on. On his return to Ephesus he began as usual by going to the synagogue and engaging in discussions there.

MALCOLM

Acts says that he was able to do that for three months but that then opposition hardened and he had to find other accommodation.[16]

ALEC

What he did was to rent a lecture-hall owned by a man named Tyrannus, where he was able to teach each day from 11 a.m. till 4 p.m., that is, during the period of the siesta.

MALCOLM

Doubtless there were a good number of slaves who wanted to listen to him, and that would have suited them well, because they would have been free at that time of day. Also, if Paul was earning his living as was his practice, it would have suited him too since he would not be working during the siesta. Hasn't it been suggested, Alec, that Paul met with a good deal more trouble during his two years at Ephesus than Acts suggests?

ALEC

Yes, some scholars think that is so, and that Paul was imprisoned here more than once. There is, for instance, that reference in one of his letters to his having fought with beasts at Ephesus:[17] he was probably speaking metaphorically. It has also been suggested that he wrote the so-called captivity letters, namely Colossians, Philippians and Philemon, here rather than during his final imprisonment at Rome, which

16. Acts 19: 8 f.   17. 1 Corinthians 15: 32.

119

however is more probable in my opinion. What can be said with confidence, though Acts doesn't mention it, is that during his time at Ephesus Paul sent one or more of his colleagues, notably Epaphras,[18] to evangelize the cities in the Lycus valley – Colossae, Laodicea and Hierapolis.

MALCOLM

Those were the ones of whom Paul said that they hadn't seen his face,[19] which must mean that he hadn't evangelized them himself, although he took an eager, indeed a fatherly, interest in them.

ALEC

Hardly anything remains of those places today. The most valuable thing that has survived from them is Paul's letter to the Colossians, which marks an important development in his thinking. Instead of talking about Jesus as the Messiah of the Jews who fulfilled the Old Testament prophecies, he now speaks of what we may call the cosmic Christ, the Christ who is the agent of God in the whole creative process, who sustains the whole universe, who, as it were, holds all things together, the principle of unity in all things.

MALCOLM

I suppose that way of presenting the truth about Christ would appeal more to the Gentiles and to the Greeks.

18. Colossians 1: 7 f. 19. Colossians 2: 1.

---

16 *'They all assembled in the theatre here and two of Paul's associates were dragged in.'* (p. 124)
17 *'But when he saw all the evidences of idolatry . . . he couldn't contain himself . . .'* (p. 111)
18 *'Great is Diana of the Ephesians!'* (p. 124)

ARTEMIS - DIANA

ALEC

Quite so. Paul also now tends to play down his expectation of the imminent end of all things and the return of Christ in glory. He stills expects this, but his emphasis now is on the present possibility of beginning already to live the life of the age to come, the risen life with Christ. Further, Paul now thinks of the Christians as the nucleus or the first-fruits of the unity of mankind in Christ, which was to be the final consummation of all things.

MALCOLM

That is the Church as the body of Christ, isn't it?

ALEC

Yes. Of course, the English word 'church' is used in a variety of senses – of buildings and of ecclesiastical organizations and of denominations and so on. For Paul it was the universal community in which all who were in Christ were bound together – a universal community which had, as it were, its local embodiments in Ephesus and Corinth and Colossae and wherever there was a company of believers. It wasn't a mere collection of individuals but a structured community in which each member had his special place and function to serve and help the others, like the various limbs in the body.

MALCOLM

I suppose that it is on this concept of Paul's of the Church as the body of Christ that the whole institutional development of Christianity is based – the creeds, the liturgies, the hier-archies, and every kind of elaboration.

ALEC

I fear those things are liable to conceal rather than reveal what the Church actually meant to Paul and the early Christians. For them an essential part of the Christian experience was being brought into a community, a common life, that transcended all the barriers that normally keep human beings apart. This is clear from what Paul wrote to the Colossians:

> *Here there cannot be Greek and Jew, circumcised and uncircumcised, barbarian, Scythian, slave, free man, but Christ is all, and in all. Put on then, as God's chosen ones, holy and beloved, compassion, kindness, lowliness, meekness, and patience, forbearing one another and, if one has a complaint against another, forgiving each other; as the Lord has forgiven you, so you also must forgive. And above all these put on love, which binds everything together in perfect harmony. And let the peace of Christ rule in your hearts, to which indeed you were called in the one body. And be thankful.*[20]

MALCOLM

Whether the letter to the Colossians was actually written here or later at Rome, I take it that all these ideas were very much in Paul's mind during his stay in Ephesus. His two years' ministry here came summarily to an end as a result of a particular row, didn't it?

ALEC

Yes, indeed. We haven't yet mentioned what was perhaps the principal thing that Ephesus was famous for – the great temple of Diana.

MALCOLM

It must have been a huge place.

ALEC

It's said to have been four times the size of the Parthenon in

20. Colossians 3 : 11–15.

Athens. People flocked here on pilgrimage. It was one of the seven wonders of the world.[21]

MALCOLM

The goddess herself was a goddess of fertility.

ALEC

Like a lot of gods and goddesses she was a conflated figure: a local deity who was identified with the Greek Artemis and the Roman Diana, but primarily, as you say, a goddess of fertility.

MALCOLM

As is evident from all the breasts with which she is portrayed.

ALEC

Which some have supposed to be dates!

MALCOLM

Of course the cult of Diana was utterly repugnant to Paul. For him the only real God was the one, holy, living, eternal Being to whom the Old Testament bore witness, the creator and sustainer of all that is, of whom it was said, 'Thou shalt have none other gods but me'. So all these pagan gods and goddesses were fantasy and folly.

In the theatre at Ephesus

ALEC

What brought Paul's stay at Ephesus to an end was that the silversmiths, who represented a very important commercial interest, got seriously troubled about the result of Paul's

21. The other six were the pyramids of Egypt, the hanging gardens at Babylon, the Colossus at Rhodes, Phidias' statue of Jupiter at Athens, the Mausoleum at Halicarnassus, and the lighthouse on the island of Pharos at Alexandria.

preaching, which in effect cut the ground from under the cult of Diana. They specialized in making silver figures of the goddess.

MALCOLM

Actually, my dear Alec, they needn't have troubled themselves, because a great deal of very much bigger business was going to come their way once the churches got really started! However, they weren't to know that.

ALEC

No. Supposing their livelihood to be threatened, they adopted the usual recourse of stirring up the mob and got them into a great state of excitement. They all assembled in the theatre here and two of Paul's associates were dragged in. But it is so vividly described in Acts that it's best to read the account there.

> *Paul wished to go in among the crowd, but the disciples would not let him in; some of the Asiarchs also [they were the provincial officials], who were friends of his, sent to him and begged him not to venture into the theatre. Now some cried one thing, some another; for the assembly was in confusion, and most of them did not know why they had come together. Some of the crowd prompted Alexander, whom the Jews had put forward [presumably to dissociate the Jews from the Christians]. And Alexander motioned with his hand, wishing to make a defence to the people. But when they recognized that he was a Jew, for about two hours they all with one voice cried out, 'Great is Diana of the Ephesians!'*[22]

MALCOLM

I love that, you know, 'Great is Diana of the Ephesians! Great is Diana of the Ephesians!' For two hours! So extraordinarily like the idiot demonstrators of our time.

22. Acts 19: 30–4

THE MARTYR

THE MARTYR

Introduction

AFTER his long stay in Ephesus, Paul first made a round of visits in Macedonia and Greece and arranged for delegates of the churches, which had been making a collection of money that was to be given to the poor Christians of Jerusalem,[1] to meet him at Troas so that they could travel together. Paul himself went overland to Assos where he joined the rest of the party on board a chartered ship. They made a stop at Miletus so that Paul could address the elders of the Ephesian church. They then sailed in easy stages for Caesarea, and from there Paul went up to Jerusalem for the last time. After the collection had been handed over to James, Paul was (mistakenly) accused of having taken a Gentile into the part of the Temple that was reserved for Jews only. In the course of the commotion that followed, Paul was taken in charge by the Roman authorities who later transferred him to Caesarea, where he was kept under arrest for two years before his decision to appeal to Caesar involved his going to Rome for trial. After an eventful voyage which ended in shipwreck, Paul at last arrived in the capital of the Empire which he had long ago determined to reach one way or another. Although still under arrest there, he was free to bear his final witness to the gospel by preaching and by martyrdom.

1. Romans 15:25 ff.; 1 Corinthians 16:1 ff.; 2 Corinthians 8:1–9: 14; Acts 24:17.

At Assos

MALCOLM

After his long stay in Ephesus, Paul was on the road again, this time making for Jerusalem.

ALEC

He had long wanted to arrange a collection from the more affluent churches for the poor Jewish Christians in Jerusalem. And he had been round visiting the churches in Macedonia and Greece to make sure that everything was in order. He arranged too that representatives of the churches should meet him at Troas to take the collection on the voyage.

MALCOLM

Then he decided that he himself would do the first bit of the journey by land and he met the others here in the old port of Assos. I should suppose he came from Troas on horseback, for I don't see how otherwise he could have made the journey in time. It's easy to imagine the boat waiting here and Paul arriving. I wonder what he was thinking about as he came along.

ALEC

He always had a tremendous lot on his mind, what he once called 'the care of all the churches'.[2] We can get a fair idea of the things that were habitually occupying his thoughts from the letters that he had already written before this time, especially the letters to the Corinthians. I like to think that the themes which were always uppermost in his mind are

2. 2 Corinthians 11: 28.

128

summed up in that sentence at the end of 2 Corinthians: 'The grace of the Lord Jesus Christ and the love of God and the fellowship of the Holy Spirit be with you all.'

MALCOLM

I suppose he may well have had too a sense of foreboding about this journey to Jerusalem which was in fact to be his last.

ALEC

That certainly comes out in the story as it is told in Acts, which is the only record we have of the voyage. There is a sense of foreboding both in Paul's own mind and in the groups of Christians whom he met on the way.

At Miletus

MALCOLM

Paul and his companions set sail from Assos and followed along the coast, putting in from time to time to meet groups of Christians. For instance, they put in here at Miletus, where the elders of the church in Ephesus came to meet them. In those days Miletus was a big and beautiful bay with a fine harbour. Although it is now a rather desolate place, curiously enough the spirit of Paul seems to me to be stronger here than almost anywhere we've been.

ALEC

I think this is because the speech that he made to the Ephesian elders is so very moving.

And now, behold, I know that all you among whom I have gone about preaching the kingdom will see my face no more. Therefore

I testify to you this day that I am innocent of the blood of all of you, for I did not shrink from declaring to you the whole counsel of God. Take heed to yourselves and to all the flock, in which the Holy Spirit has made you guardians, to feed the church of the Lord which he obtained with his own blood. I know that after my departure fierce wolves will come in among you, not sparing the flock; and from among your own selves will arise men speaking perverse things, to draw away the disciples after them. Therefore be alert, remembering that for three years I did not cease night or day to admonish every one with tears. And now I commend you to God and to the word of his grace, which is able to build you up and give you the inheritance among all those who are sanctified. I coveted no one's silver or gold or apparel. You yourselves know that these hands ministered to my necessities, and to those who were with me. In all things I have shown you that by so toiling one must help the weak, remembering the words of the Lord Jesus, how he said, 'It is more blessed to give than to receive'.[3]

Acts adds that 'when he had spoken thus, he knelt down and prayed with them all. And they all wept and embraced Paul and kissed him, sorrowing most of all because of the word he had spoken, that they should see his face no more. And they brought him to the ship.'[4]

At Jerusalem

MALCOLM

They landed at Caesarea and then had the overland journey to Jerusalem.

3. Acts 20: 25–35.
4. Acts 20: 36 ff.

ALEC

It had been quite a long sea voyage, and they put in at various ports, notably at Tyre where there was a poignant farewell to the local Christians on the beach.

MALCOLM

And so at last they arrived at their destination, Jerusalem. This was the last time that Paul's eyes were to rest on the holy city which had for him so many mixed associations.

ALEC

I always suppose that no Jew could ever approach Jerusalem without a quickening of the pulse.

MALCOLM

I'm sure that's true, considering the fantastic part it had played in their history and in the scriptures. At the same time, from Paul's point of view it involved the prospect of a row, because every time he came to Jerusalem there was trouble.

ALEC

But remember that this time he had got a handsome collection to present to the Jewish Christians and surely that would create a favourable atmosphere; or he could reasonably hope so.

MALCOLM

Alec, I think he knew his fellow countrymen pretty well, and he knew that when he handed over the collection, the prospect of a row would be just as serious as ever.

ALEC

On this occasion he was prepared to go further than he had before. When James had a meeting with him, Paul agreed to pay the expenses of some Jewish Christians who had made a vow. That was going a long way to compromise his ordinary attitude to the Law and the strict customs of Judaism. It was a very friendly gesture.

MALCOLM

It was a gesture that also involved a good deal of the duplicity which I seem to detect in his whole attitude to this matter. When he was with the Gentiles and in churches away from Jerusalem, he took a very free and easy attitude to Jewish orthodoxy. But when he was here in Jerusalem he tended to be – one might almost say he masqueraded as – a very strict Jew.

ALEC

I wouldn't myself use the words duplicity or masquerade. It was his principle to go as far as he could always to meet those to whom he was speaking. He said himself: 'To the Jews I became as a Jew, in order to win Jews ... to those outside the law I became as one outside the law ... that I might win those outside the law. . . . I have become all things to all men.'[5] This was his principle, in order to hold together in the one Church both Jewish and Gentile Christians.

MALCOLM

A sort of St Machiavelli.

ALEC

No, not Machiavelli. You always use loaded expressions. This is a very good, splendid kind of inconsistency which only a man who lives by the Spirit, and not by rigid adherence to law, can compass.

5. 1 Corinthians 9: 20 ff.

MALCOLM

Anyway, it didn't prevent the row, because that broke out as fiercely as ever, didn't it?

ALEC

Yes, but it wasn't caused by the Jewish Christians. Some Jews from Ephesus, who were up in Jerusalem on pilgrimage, recognized Paul and quite untruly accused him of having taken a Gentile Christian into the inner court of the Temple, which was reserved exclusively for Jews. They started a terrific hullabaloo about it. Paul was dragged out of the Temple, and the mob was going to lynch him.

MALCOLM

But fortunately the Roman authorities intervened and he was taken into the nearby barracks.

ALEC

Yes, and this time Paul took advantage of his Roman citizenship. The centurion in charge therefore treated him with much respect.

MALCOLM

And took steps to remove him to Caesarea where the Roman governor resided and where the case could be dealt with in a calmer atmosphere.

At Caesarea

MALCOLM

I wonder, Alec, if you agree with me that there's something rather depressing about these ruins. We are told that this was the governor's palace where Paul was brought before him, but, unless one happens to be an archaeologist, what does it signify? All one sees is just stones piled up and the people maundering round day after day, rather disconsolately, trying to be interested, seeing them only as stones. It's a sort of twentieth-century totem, I think.

ALEC

I must confess that to me one ruin is much like another, with certain notable exceptions of course. But I can't say that this is one. When Paul got here, the Jewish high priest and other leaders of the Jews soon came down from Jerusalem, bringing with them a smart lawyer, named Tertullus. The lawyer stated the Jewish case before Felix the governor, and then Paul very effectively conducted his own defence – so effectively that the governor could see nothing to condemn him for and so simply kept him in preventive detention with access to his friends.

MALCOLM

His normal activities don't seem to have been impeded. I imagine there was a Christian church here.

ALEC

We know about Philip and his four prophetic daughters who lived in Caesarea.[6] No doubt they among others attended to Paul's needs. I should think he had quite an agreeable time here.

MALCOLM

And had people with him. Luke was here, wasn't he?

6. Acts 21:8 f.

ALEC

So it seems, if he was the author of the so-called 'we' passages in Acts, the kind of travel diary that is incorporated in the book. Some people think that it was during this period that Luke got a lot of information both for the Acts of the Apostles and for his Gospel. I'm rather dubious about this myself, but it is a possible view.

MALCOLM

If Luke was with Paul for two years here in Caesarea collecting information for the Acts of the Apostles, then I don't think he did particularly well. But then after all Luke was a doctor, and doctors are not usually very literate, are they?

ALEC

I wouldn't agree about that altogether, though I know who you are thinking about!

MALCOLM

Anyhow, Paul's case remained in abeyance, and there's a strong suggestion in Acts that the governor hoped during that time that some financial arrangement would be forthcoming.

ALEC

Yes, it says that Felix used to call for Paul occasionally and hoped that he would receive a bribe.[7]

MALCOLM

So this much-boosted inflexible Roman justice, even at the level of a governor, was corrupt.

7. Acts 24: 26.

ALEC

I'm afraid that is so. But other governments have been subject to similar temptations.

MALCOLM

One's heard of it in our own day. The next thing that happened was that the governor changed, didn't he? There was a new governor.

ALEC

After two years Felix was relieved, and Porcius Festus arrived to succeed him. And then the Jews thought they had got a chance of starting the case again. However, Festus wasn't impressed by their case, and if Paul had not at this juncture made the decision to appeal to Caesar, which he was entitled to do as a Roman citizen, he might have been released.

MALCOLM

But the appeal to Caesar meant that he had to be sent to Rome.

ALEC

Exactly.

MALCOLM

So now the die was cast. And Paul plus his escort plus some of

---

19 '. . . he met the others here in the old port of Assos.' (p. 128)
20 'This was the last time that Paul's eyes were to rest on the holy city . . .' (p. 131)
21 'So now the die was cast. And Paul . . . set sail from Caesarea for Italy.' (p. 137)

his companions, probably Luke, and some other prisoners, set sail from Caesarea for Italy.

ALEC
Let's see what Acts says about it.

And when it was decided that we should sail for Italy, they delivered Paul and some other prisoners to a centurion of the Augustan Cohort, named Julius. And embarking in a ship of Adramyttium, which was about to sail to the ports along the coast of Asia, we put to sea, accompanied by Aristarchus, a Macedonian from Thessalonica.[8]

They called at various ports along the way until they got to Myra, where the centurion was able to transfer them to a bigger ship from Alexandria which was no doubt laden with grain for Rome.

In Crete

MALCOLM
The ship sailed along the coast of Crete, and put in at a place called Fair Havens.

ALEC
And it is still called that today.

MALCOLM
Now wasn't there a controversy about staying or going on?

8. Acts 27: 1 ff.

ALEC

Paul, who was a very experienced traveller both by land and sea, gave as his advice that they should stay here in view of the time of year. But the majority, that is the owner and the captain and the centurion, and perhaps some others who were consulted, were in favour of trying to get on.

MALCOLM

They wanted to go further along the coast and winter in a more suitable harbour, but Paul was insistent that the right thing to do was to spend the winter here. And how right he proved!

ALEC

Yes, although they had favourable winds to start with, a tremendous north-easter blew up very quickly and took them right off their course, with the result that ultimately they were wrecked off the coast of Malta. The boat was broken up but the passengers and crew, who are said to have numbered nearly three hundred, got ashore all right, and were made to feel at home by the islanders. As it was now winter they had to stay for three months, but as soon as the sailing season re-opened in February or March they set sail for Italy in a ship named *Castor and Pollux*.

On the Appian Way

MALCOLM

Here we are at last in Italy and on the old Appian Way which Paul took to Rome.

ALEC

Paul and his companions were met at a place agreeably called 'Three Taverns' by a party of Christians from Rome who had come out to welcome them.

MALCOLM

I presume that this party consisted of some of those who are mentioned in the last chapter of the Epistle to the Romans.

ALEC

Surely: they were no doubt converts of his who had got to Rome before him. Obviously Paul was much cheered by this welcome, because it says in Acts that, when he met his fellow Christians, he thanked God and took courage. That implies that he had had some trepidation beforehand, but now he must have entered Rome with great joy and confidence.

On the roof of St Peter's

MALCOLM

Now that we've come to the last phase of Paul's life, it's a natural thing to come up here on to the roof of St Peter's basilica and look down on this great square, where many groups of pilgrims are assembling as we watch, in order to enter and worship. After all, this is the centre of Western Christianity. Each of these people, interminably climbing up the steps, is doing so because of these journeys of Paul that we've been following, isn't that so?

ALEC

In a sense you can say that this is Paul's Rome as much as it is Peter's. But very little of Paul's Rome actually survives. We don't even know where he resided, though of course there are traditional locations.

MALCOLM

And yet this great ecclesiastical structure, this enormous organization, is the fruit of his life. What on earth would Paul think of it? What, for example, would he think of the great services that take place in St Peter's with the most extraordinarily beautiful ceremonial and music and vestments and all that? Would Paul recognize it as the outcome of his life and labours if we could get him in there just to see a high mass? Would he instinctively recognize that it was the same thing as the meal which they took in common together, the Lord's Supper?

ALEC

If you press the question, I should say, Yes. They still use, here as elsewhere, the very words that Paul gave to the Corinthians in telling them to do it, and they perform the same actions though in a much more elaborate and stylized setting.

MALCOLM

We can be sure that in Rome Paul continued to write his letters. There's that one that is the shortest but also in some ways the most delightful – the letter to Philemon.

ALEC

That was almost certainly written from Rome, and it is perhaps the most charming private letter that has come down to us from antiquity.

MALCOLM

And the subject matter is extremely interesting.

ALEC

What happened was that he met in Rome an escaped slave, named Onesimus. He obviously loved him and also much enjoyed his company and his services. But he told the slave that it was his duty to go back to his master. So Paul wrote in his letter to Philemon:

Though I am bold enough in Christ to command you to do what is required, yet for love's sake I prefer to appeal to you – I, Paul, an old man and now a prisoner also for Christ Jesus – I appeal to you for my child, Onesimus, whose father I have become in my imprisonment. (Formerly he was useless to you, but now he is indeed useful to you and to me.) I am sending him back to you, sending my very heart. I would have been glad to keep him with me, in order that he might serve me on your behalf during my imprisonment for the gospel; but I preferred to do nothing without your consent in order that your goodness might not be by compulsion but of your own free will.[9]

It is clear from this letter that Paul did not call in question the institution of slavery, as it then existed in the pagan world. From his point of view Onesimus had done wrong in running away from his master. The institution of slavery was of course taken for granted in the world then and for long afterwards. But Paul's teaching had the effect of humanizing it, as we see from this letter, and in the long run his teaching undermined it. For he taught that in Christ all are one and equal; there is neither bond nor free: 'for you are all one in Christ Jesus'.[10]

MALCOLM

Supposing Paul was up here with us now and looking down at all these people, what would he think? They are still en-

9. Philemon 8–14.   10. Galatians 3 : 28.

slaved. They've still got their law on which they pride themselves. The silversmiths are still busy. And yet I have an idea
that he would feel about them as he did in his life-time, this
great love and sense of oneness with his fellows, and joy too
that they should still be climbing up these steps to enter and
kneel down and worship.

In the cloisters of St Paul's outside the Walls

MALCOLM

Our long and arduous journey ends here, at Paul's reputed
burial place. I say long and arduous for us, but for him how
much longer and how much more arduous!

ALEC

There is no definite information about the exact circumstances of Paul's death and burial. The probability is that he
was executed, martyred, under Nero as a disturber of the
peace, and of course if they had wanted evidence that he had
been a disturber of the peace, they could easily have got it
from many cities in the Empire.

MALCOLM

My goodness, I can't imagine an easier task! I find it rather
difficult to form a picture of what Paul's life in Rome was
like when he was here at the end of his days.

ALEC

It must have been a very easy form of house arrest because he
was free to see people, to preach and do more or less what he

liked. Of course he had no desire to escape – they could see that. He was only too thankful to be in Rome at last.

MALCOLM

Though he speaks of being bound with a chain, doesn't he?

ALEC

Many people have been puzzled by the fact that the Acts of the Apostles, which was written perhaps twenty years or so after his death makes no mention of it, although the author and his readers must have known about it. But I think the explanation is fairly simple. From their point of view, Paul's death wasn't the culmination of his life. It was inevitable of course that he should die sooner or later and indeed be martyred, but the culmination or climax was the fact that he was free at last to proclaim the gospel in Rome. An alternative title for the Acts of the Apostles might have been 'From Jerusalem to Rome'. It starts with the Christian movement as a tiny handful of dispirited men, in an obscure province of the Empire, outside Jerusalem, and now, thirty years or so later, it has spread all round the Mediterranean world, and here to crown the story is the great apostle of the Gentiles, free to proclaim the gospel and to preach in the capital of the world itself, in Rome, quite openly and without any hindrance. It is interesting that the last word in Acts in the Greek is an adverb meaning 'without hindrance'. And when we recall how many hindrances he had encountered in the course of his voyages and travels, we can see how this was indeed the climax and a triumphant conclusion.

MALCOLM

'From Jerusalem to Rome', I like that. That might almost be the title of what we've been trying to do. Alec, when we set out in Tarsus, you said you were sure that following these journeys of Paul in the light of his own writings and of the Acts would give us a clearer picture of what he was and what he did and what he believed. Now I can say with the utmost truth and sincerity that, as far as I am concerned, that is so.

Of course there are all sorts of questions that have arisen. Who wrote the Acts of the Apostles? Was it Luke? What degree of credibility attaches to it? When was this letter or that letter written? All these things have arisen and I don't feel competent to have any particular opinion on them or even, if I'm to be truthful, any particular interest in them. I can somehow see a distinction between meaning and truth, between historicity and reality. But that's beside the point.

What has emerged for me is a clear picture of this man, the sort of person he was, the sort of life he lived, the utter dedication to truth which governed every action, every minute, of his days. This light that he'd seen and that he spread, and that he shone continuously, whatever his mood might be. If I were to pinpoint the whole thing to one single passage, it would be this one:

> *Who shall separate us from the love of Christ? shall tribulation, or distress, or persecution, or famine, or nakedness, or peril, or sword? . . . Nay, in all these things we are more than conquerors through him that loved us. For I am persuaded, that neither death, nor life, nor angels, nor principalities, nor powers, nor things present, nor things to come, nor height, nor depth, nor any other creature, shall be able to separate us from the love of God, which is in Christ Jesus our Lord.*[11]

11. Romans 8: 35–9.

EPILOGUE

by *Alec Vidler*

M Y earliest impressions of Paul, if I may put it so, were far from favourable. They date from the time when as a young boy I was taken to church and had to listen, or appear to listen, to what seemed to be very boring sermons. Apart from their general incomprehensibility to my youthful mind, I recall that our vicar, whom later on I came to admire, was not only in the habit of including in his discourses long extracts from the previous Saturday's religious article in *The Times* newspaper, but he – and his curates too – were constantly talking about 'St Paul', whoever he may have been, and quoting things that he had said. I could make nothing of what these quotations were about, nor could I understand why such a fuss was made about 'St Paul'. I still consider that his letters (or epistles) should be read by adults, not by children. The case is different with his adventures which are related in the Acts of the Apostles, though my recollection is that his missionary journeys, which we had to study at school with examinations in view, did not overcome my aversion to the mention of his name.

It was not until I began to study theology as an under-graduate at Cambridge that I began to see why Paul was a very important person, both on his own account and because of what he achieved. Even so, having to wrestle with the Greek text of his more difficult letters, and having to satisfy examiners that I had got the measure of the many knotty problems they present, was calculated to strengthen my initial resistance to falling under his spell. Although from then onwards it was my business to familiarize myself with his 'life and letters', and although I now realized of course that he had given utterance to sublime thoughts, the fact is that for many years I devoted much more time and enthusiasm to the writings of St John which for a number of reasons made a singular appeal to me.

A turning-point or a decisive stage in my attitude to Paul came when at last I saw, or thought I saw, what he was driving at in his teaching about 'justification by faith'. I had known about this previously as an abstract or theoretical doctrine, but it did not really get under my skin or strike me as of immense practical importance until the 1930s when I was already approaching middle age.

It must be remembered that the First World War, which might have been expected to impress on all who experienced it the sombre, indeed tragic, character of human existence and the precariousness of what is called 'civilization', was in fact succeeded, not least in Britain, by a mood of confident idealism, of secular optimism, and of utopianism. English Christians were certainly influenced by this mood and to a considerable extent reflected it. That was so in my own case, although I did not for long find the rhetoric about progress convincing. But it took me some time to see through the fallacies contained in such statements as that, if only all men would live up to the ideals set forth in the Sermon on the Mount, the kingdom of God would come on earth.

The time did, however, come when I started to distrust every sentence that began with the words 'if only'. I saw that the heart of the Christian gospel was not in the Sermon on

the Mount, marvellous as that is, but in what Paul had proclaimed about salvation or 'justification' by faith and by
grace. It came home to me that, especially in his letters to the
Galatians and Romans, he had plumbed the depths of the
human condition – not only of my own condition, but of
the needs and dilemmas of mankind as a whole.

To put the matter as simply as possible, I now realized –
what hitherto I had paid only lip-service to – that men are
incapable of putting themselves right with the all-holy God,
or of justifying themselves, by anything that they can do.
They cannot save themselves, still less save the world or bring
in the kingdom of God, however hard they try. When Paul
said that 'a man is not justified by works of the law but through
faith in Jesus Christ'[1] what he said was true, not only of
the works or good deeds prescribed by the Jewish Law, but
of any conceivable scheme by which men imagined they
could perfect themselves and put the world to rights.

Although men are not totally corrupt in the sense that they
are incapable of doing any good at all – it would be absurd to
say that – the truth is that the best of men and their best accom-
plishments are tainted or poisoned at the core by their pride
or egotism or self-centredness, however fair they may look
from outside. I once stated what I believed to be the presup-
position of Paul's understanding of Christianity in the
following passage:

> *Christianity . . . does not say that, in spite of appearances, we are*
> *all murderers or burglars or crooks or sexual perverts at heart;*
> *it does not say that we are totally depraved, in the sense that we*
> *are incapable of feeling or responding to any good impulses*
> *whatever. The truth is much deeper and more subtle than that.*
> *It is precisely when you consider the* best *in man that you see*

1. Galatians 2: 16.

147

there is in each of us a hard core of pride or self-centredness which corrupts our best achievements and blights our best experiences. It comes out in all sorts of ways – in the jealousy which spoils our friendships, in the vanity we feel when we have done something pretty good, in the easy conversion of love into lust, in the meanness which makes us depreciate the efforts of other people, in the distortion of our own judgement by our own self-interest, in our fondness for flattery and our resentment of blame, in our self-assertive profession of fine ideals which we never begin to practise . . .[2]

The human condition is in fact worse than that. Not only are all men guilty but they belong to a guilty race. Collective man is worse than individual men. Individuals can blush and feel ashamed but, as Coleridge said, 'multitudes never blush'. They do horrible things with an easy conscience from which the individuals who compose them would shrink. This truth was stated with devastating effect in a book entitled *Moral Man and Immoral Society* by Reinhold Neibuhr, published in 1932. Niebuhr was one of the theologians who helped me most to appreciate Paul's message. Another was the British theologian, P. T. Forsyth, who had been prophesying hard and unpopular things before, during and after the First World War, and also proclaiming God's remedy for man's guilt. At this time I learned a lot too from some of the German Lutheran pastors who had come to England as a result of the Nazi persecution. Luther's own writings open doors into the inner recesses of Paul's teaching.

Anyhow, it came to me, with the force of a revelation, that man is basically incapable of saving himself or putting himself right, and that is why it is good news (which is what

2. *Secular Despair and Christian Faith* (1941), p. 22.

'gospel' means) that God sent his Son into the world to save the world, and to give all who will accept this good news a new start in life. For to receive Jesus Christ as Saviour is to be assured that you are made right with God (or 'justified') not by anything you can do or by any merits you can acquire, but purely as a result of his most generous initiative. While you are still a sinner, you are welcomed, as the prodigal son was, into the new humanity and the new community of which Jesus Christ is the Head and the Centre.

This new humanity and this new community – which Paul calls the body of Christ – is in this world, like the body of Jesus on the cross, right in the thick of the conflicts of history, battered about, a laughing-stock at first sight. It will be seen in its glory not here but beyond history, when it is unveiled in the final resurrection and in the consummation of all things. Yet even now, we belong to Christ and his glorious body. We can at least *taste* its presence and its power. We can know the beginnings of the 'fellowship of the Holy Spirit'. We can take our part in the struggles and conflicts of this world as men whose true home is in another world, and who at the same time have in this world to prove their faith, and who know to whom they belong.

Christians will do all the good they can, both individually and socially, out of gratitude for what God has already done for them and through his Spirit at work in them, but not with any idea that they are earning a reward or with any pretentious claim that they are creating a new world. 'Justification by faith' or salvation by the grace of God does not mean that man's good works are of no account. Far from it. Observe how Paul, in his famous exposition of justification by faith in his letter to the Romans, when in the first eleven chapters he has blown sky high the whole idea of men's justifying themselves by good works, nevertheless turns round in the twelfth and following chapters and says in effect: 'Now that you have been justified freely by the grace of God, therefore present your bodies as a living sacrifice . . .', and he gives a very practical account of what it means to live as members of Christ in this world.

I would only add that, just as Paul in this same letter to the Romans looked forward to the eventual salvation of those who at present rejected or did not acknowledge Christ as Saviour, so it is that salvation by faith does not entail the belief that only professing Christians can be saved or get right with God. I agree with a Roman Catholic theologian who has recently said:

> *Among men whom the explicit message of Christ or of the Old Testament has not yet reached – in all those searching sincerely for what is good, just, honest, and true, and dedicating themselves to what they understand to be the absolute demand of love and justice – there can already be operating 'salvation through faith'.*[3]

Broadly speaking, it was these cardinal elements in Paul's teaching that won me to him in the 1930s and 1940s. During the succeeding years I came to realize that there is an inexhaustible amount of further truth to be discovered in his letters. It does not for the most part lie on the surface: it has to be dug out. Moreover, while the letters contain passages of unforgettable eloquence, they also contain a good deal that remains obscure, even in a modern translation and after commentators have done all they can, and there are also in

3. Bernard Häring in *Theology and Church in Times of Change* (1970), p. 62.

Paul's letters things that were of only temporary interest or application.

For example, his attempt in 1 Corinthians 11:2–16 to rationalize on lofty theological grounds the social convention which required women to be veiled is far-fetched and quite unconvincing, as in the end he himself had to acknowledge. That is to say, not everything that Paul wrote is of equal value for us. How should it be, in view of the fact that he was addressing himself to immediate and practical questions, and not indulging in timeless speculations? Even so, there is more than enough in his letters to provide anyone with a life-time's food for thought and meditation and for the enlightenment that comes through reading, marking and inwardly digesting.

All this had been borne in upon me over the years and well before I received the unexpected invitation to accompany Malcolm Muggeridge upon the exploratory journey which led, among other things, to the production of this book. I ask myself now what I have learned about Paul as a result of this unforeseen opportunity of following the course of his travels, and of reflecting on his experiences, his achievements and his witness to truth in the actual places where they originated. It was not only our time out in the Middle East that I found rewarding, but also the months of preparation during which I engaged in a renewed study of Paul's letters and of the literature about him. (I may remark here, in passing, that both Malcolm and I found that of the innumerable books that have been written about Paul, the two most discerning and most useful were: Adolf Deissmann's *St Paul: a study in social and religious history*[4] and A. D. Nock's *St Paul.*)[5]

4. English translation, published by Hodder and Stoughton (1912); paperback edition published by Harper & Row (1957).

5. Home University Library (1938).

First, I was confirmed in my belief that there is an in-exhaustible amount of truth to be discovered in Paul's letters.

Secondly, I feel now that I had not previously realized how *extraordinary* his character and his achievements were, and also how stupendous was his courage and how dauntless his dedication to the truth that he knew himself to be bound to proclaim. After all, the Acts of the Apostles gives only a fragmentary account of the ordeals and hazards that Paul had to face. Contrast the comparatively little that it tells us with what Paul himself incidentally mentions in his second letter to the Corinthians: he is saying how he had undergone far more imprisonments than his critics, 'with countless beatings, and often near death'.

Five times I have received at the hands of the Jews the forty lashes less one. Three times I have been beaten with rods; once I was stoned. Three times I have been shipwrecked; a night and a day I have been adrift at sea. . . .[6]

That leads to a third thing that became much clearer to me, namely that to get at the heart of what Paul stood for and what made him tick we must depend on his genuine letters rather than on the Acts of the Apostles, though that provides an invaluable framework for the story of his life. In Paul's

6. 2 Corinthians 11:23–8; the whole passage should be read.

---

22 '*Here we are at last in Italy and on the old Appian Way which Paul took to Rome.*' (p. 138)
23 '*Our long and arduous journey ends here, at Paul's reputed burial place.*' (p. 142)
24 '*Who shall separate us from the love of Christ?*' (p. 144)

letters we are in direct contact with the original source of the Christian movement, much more so than in the case of most other New Testament writings.[7] Acts, in particular, while it is a skilful composition and a splendid piece of literature,[8] was written long after the events it records in the light of such information as was available to the author which he interpreted to the best of his ability. But it is notorious that some of the statements in Acts, e.g. about Paul's visits to Jerusalem, are inconsistent with what he himself tells us in his letters. Ingenious scholars have gone to great lengths to iron out the differences, but in my opinion these earnest endeavours are unnecessary. We should accept Paul's own testimony and admit that Acts can be in error. In any case questions of this sort have very little bearing on the heart of the matter.

But fourthly, while I retract nothing that I have so far said about Paul, it has been borne in upon me as never before that, if I am to be honest, by temperament he is not congenial to me. Although he obviously had a mind of exceptional power and was adept at arguing in the manner of the rabbis, yet fundamentally he was an intuitive thinker. He had the insights of a seer and was able to express what he saw with the confidence of a prophet and with the imaginative resourcefulness of a poet. It has been well said that 'to speak about God with any degree of adequacy one must be a poet or

7. By Paul's 'genuine letters' I mean Galatians, 1 and 2 Thessalonians, Romans, 1 and 2 Corinthians, Colossians, Philippians, and Philemon. While Ephesians, 1 and 2 Timothy, and Titus probably contain nuggets from Paul himself, they have been written up or recast by Paul's followers in accordance with a literary convention of the time.

8. To get its full effect, it should be read through at a sitting, as can easily be done on a wet Sunday afternoon.

prophet or mystic'. Paul, like other poets, prophets and mystics, had scant regard for the niceties of logic or of rational coherence. He never used words like 'possibly', 'probably' or 'perhaps'.

In this respect, and maybe in others also, Malcolm's temperament or – I would say – his genius resembles Paul's. I, on the other hand, have always regarded probability as the guide of life and have the academic or donnish proclivity for weighing pros and cons and reaching hesitant conclusions. I am not one of those who, in the words of Henry James, 'can arrive at serene conclusions without disagreeable processes'. I cannot help assuming that, to quote another American author, 'a reasonable man in any field of inquiry can be recognized by the care with which he formulates his judgments so that they might be understood and rationally assessed. Moreover, he will invariably qualify his judgments and so indicate the degree of assurance he thinks properly attaches to them.' On this showing, Paul should not be described as 'a reasonable man'. On the other hand, I also hold that there is very much about what is most important in life to be learned from non-reasonable men, and I by no means pride myself on my painfully reasonable disposition. Certainly, I have derived immense benefit from friendly commerce with minds that are differently constituted.

Thus, for instance, I learned much at one period of my life – not least in regard to the understanding of Paul – from my friend, the late D. R. Davies,[9] though I always found his sweeping assertions and confident generalizations provoking. Even more so, for over fifty years now, I have been influenced in all sorts of ways by Malcolm Muggeridge, though my

9. See his books *On to Orthodoxy* (1939) and *Down Peacock's Feathers* (1942) and his autobiography, *In Search of Myself* (1961).

154

pedestrian mentality has frequently wanted to qualify the fascinating manner in which he expresses his penetrating perceptions. Richard Simpson, Lord Acton's friend and collaborator, once wrote to him: 'You are the first man I have ever worked with, with whom I could entirely sympathize; and yet we are quite different, and only agree in the end we propose to ourselves.' I could say something very like that to Malcolm. But what concerns us here is that we are entirely at one in our sense of indebtedness to Paul. Thanks be to God.

Prayer

Oh! blessed soul of St Paul, exalted immeasurably in the Spirit, but ever sober in self-forgetfulness and devotion, that didst dare to believe in the redemption of a world through the knots of simple and unregarded folk that gathered to thy call in the purlieus of mighty cities, thou hast taught us the simplicity of that faith by which alone the world can be made, without which it is ever being unmade. A. L. LILLEY

Acknowledgments

The maps were drawn by John Flower and T. Stalker Miller, M.S.I.A.

Scripture quotations from the Revised Standard Version of the Bible, copyrighted 1946 and 1952 by the Division of Christian Education of the National Council of the Churches of Christ in the United States of America, are used by permission.

The dialogue between Peter Cook and Dudley Moore reproduced in 'Variations on a Theme' is from *Dud and Pete* by Peter Cook and Dudley Moore, published by Methuen & Co. Ltd.